Beauty

The Value of Values

BEAUTY

The Value of Values

FREDERICK TURNER

University Press of Virginia
Charlottesville and London

THE UNIVERSITY PRESS OF VIRGINIA
Copyright © 1991 by the Rector and Visitors
of the University of Virginia

First published 1991

Library of Congress Cataloging-in-Publication Data

Turner, Frederick, 1943–
Beauty : the value of values / Frederick Turner.
p.   cm.
Includes index.
ISBN 0-8139-1357-8 (cloth)
1. Aesthetics.   2. Values.   I. Title.
BH39.T87   1992
111'.85—dc20   91-22536
                                                            CIP

Printed in the United States of America

Contents

Preface

THIS BOOK is the result of a combination of a lifelong interest, a conversation, and a commission.

The lifelong interest is my own obsession with the place of beauty in the physical world and its nature as a philosophical entity; this interest was first awakened by my parents, Vic and Edie Turner, taught to know itself by my remarkable teacher John Armstrong, nurtured by J. I. M. Stewart and Helen Gardner, and given the material to build with by J. T. Fraser and the International Society for the Study of Time. It found a community in the Werner Reimers Stiftung research group on the biological foundations of beauty and a field of action in the controversial poetic transformation known sometimes as the Expansive Movement.

The conversation is an exchange of ideas that has been going on in the last five years at my own academic institution, the School of Arts and Humanities at the University of Texas at Dallas. Here a group of thinkers, brought together in part by the performance scholar Robert Corrigan, has been reexamining the roots of the humanities. Outside the University of Texas, Tom Scheff, Roy Wagner, James Hans, Robin Fox, and Robert Kellogg have also been for me important voices in the conversation; though to cite all the extraordinary people whose insights have influenced this book would tax the reader's patience.

The commission was by Nancy Essig, Director of the University Press of Virginia, to publish a pair of books, one poetry, the other prose, that would approach the same nexus of ideas in two different modes. This is the prose book; the poetry book, which should be regarded as complementary to it, is entitled *April Wind*.

Acknowledgments

Chapter 3, "The Biology of Beauty," first appeared in *Zone 6: Incorporations*, Jonathan Crary and Sanford Kwinter, eds. (New York: Zone Books, 1991). Chapter 9, "Beauty and the Anima Mundi," first appeared in *Philosophica, 1991*. The author wishes to thank the editors of these periodicals.

The quotation from Thomas Mann in chapter 3 is taken from *The Magic Mountain,* translated by H. T. Lowe-Porter, copyright 1927 and renewed 1955 by Alfred A. Knopf, Inc. Copyright 1952 by Thomas Mann. Reprinted by permission of the publisher and by permission of Martin Secker and Warburg Limited.

The quotation from Miklós Radnóti in chapter 1 is taken from the sequence "Calendar" in *Foamy Sky: The Major Poems of Miklós Radnóti,* translated by Zsuzsanna Ozsvath and Frederick Turner (Princeton: Princeton Univ. Press, Lockert Library of Poetry in Translation, 1992), by permission of the publisher.

BEAUTY
The Value of Values

One

The Experience of Beauty

THE WORD *beauty* is a little embarrassing; there is something old-fashioned about it, like a country girl wearing her mother's dress. It is precisely for this reason that I shall use it rather than the much cooler and more stylish term *the aesthetic*. *The aesthetic* is often either a euphemism for that coarse and lachrymose old *beauty* or a hard, free, clean and cruel substitute for it, steel flowers for the bride.

Not but what there is indeed a shiver of the strange in the experience of beauty—and here the reader will permit me to begin a vague and mixed list of descriptions of that experience—but it is a strangeness that lies in and beyond the acceptance of embarrassment, not in a denial of it. Take, for instance—and only examples can bring the real experience to mind—the passage in Lady Murasaki's *Genji* when the shining prince rides by the ruined palace-pavilion of the princess Suyetsumu, its roofs broken by storms, its dusty elegant apartments drifted with moonlit snow, its beautiful occupant attended only by the grotesque old court ladies of another era.

But the strangeness of beauty is always attended by a feeling of reminiscence and recognition. The palace in the tangled woods in *Genji* is, after all, a version of the universal old fairy tale of the sleeping beauty in her overgrown castle. Some years ago I bought a set of simple stoneware in a Cretan market, very irregular in form, glazed white with an easy loose pattern of little dark-blue and black arabesques. I bought it from the potters themselves, a dark blond couple, and haggled over the price because the process itself in

Greece establishes a human value for a purchase. The stoneware is distinctly odd, but its cups, its jug, its plates look like archetypal cups and jugs and plates, with a generous but simple roundness of bottom made for the comfortable containing of liquid or crumb. It is beautiful in its old strange familiarity, its match with human kinetic expectations and capacities, its friendliness to the leverage of the arm and hand and nervous system. A good typeface has the same beautiful familiarity, even when the language is one unknown to us, say Japanese or Arabic or Sanskrit.

A beautiful thing, though simple in its immediate presence, always gives us a sense of depth below depth, almost an innocent wild vertigo as one falls through its levels. Complexity is contained within simplicity, as those strange extra dimensions in superstring theory are contained, tightly coiled or packed, inside each point of threespace. Consider for example an *Embarkation for Cythera* by Poussin or Claude; the delicate leaves of the mimosa in the foreground, backlighted by the setting sun; the small figures on their way to the shadowy ship in the near middle distance; the temple and the sea-cave in the far middle distance; and the horizon, a pool of light glimmering through the glazes, beneath the stretched-out evening sky. Though the scene is utterly familiar, even stereotyped, the ratios of perspective, aerial and geometrical, with a thousand little variations and trompes l'oeil, suggest to us with a shock to the heart that we too might board that ship and sail away forever into that golden evening, that landscape of islands and distant volcanoes as familiar and terrifying as sex is to a virgin boy or girl.

Beauty has about it the quality of inexhaustibility, of depth. It connects to where we are, and indeed evokes our whole past, both of the nursery and of the race—that parkland our ancestors inhabited, where you could look out from the edge of a wood across a well-watered plain—but it also goes on from that ancient place to some new and transforming experience, something shaped though limitless. Real landscapes—say, the clouds over the Cascades seen from a plane—have the same internal depth. Some unending fractal algorithm generated the clouds, whose every detail is itself filled with detail according to an obscure scaling principle; likewise the forests, where the great inverted v's of the ridges are echoed in each little peak and cleft, and then reechoed in the shape of individual trees, boughs, tufts of foliage, needle-sprays; and the snows, in fields and swathes and splotches and jags and flashes. There is something of this delight in the stitching of a good shirt or suit. You can never get to the bottom of something beautiful, because it always finds space inside itself for a new and surprising recapitulation of its idea that adds fresh feeling to the familiar pattern.

But though it is inexhaustible, one cannot hold on to beauty very long. In Shakespeare's Sonnet 18, which is both an example and an analysis of beauty, there is the line "Rough winds do shake the darling buds of May," which catches exactly this elusiveness and transiency; summer's lease hath all too short a date. There is always a quality in beauty of "almost but not quite," of "this, but beyond," of some aching thirst at the very heart of satisfaction. Death is both the mother and the daughter of beauty.

Beauty can almost be *defined* as an absence of the desire for power, possession, success, political victory in themselves. But it is more than just the relaxation from and forgetting of the stress and tedium of power. As Pindar knew, the Olympic athlete at the moment of victory is glitteringly beautiful; the perfection of a martial art, especially as one feels it in oneself in the completion of a well-turned technique, is beautiful. But there is a "giving-away" in beauty, a sense of nothing to lose, a sense of pathos and also sufficiency in being a contender, caught well in the film *Chariots of Fire*. Defeat can be as beautiful as, perhaps more beautiful than, victory; or perhaps we could say that a beautiful victory is one in which the victor also feels the defeat of the opponent as though it were his or her own.

The mere possession of beautiful objects does not necessarily give the feeling of beauty. In fact one may need the crisis of loss to recognize the beauty of one's few beloved possessions. Beauty is not conferred or defined by social privilege and is banished at once by the paranoia of certain kinds of political partisanship. There is a beauty in the solidarity of the embattled trade union or tribal remnant defending its Masada; but that beauty turns to ugliness when one of the enemy is caught and dragged to the camp. Beauty is inversely proportional to the old seven deadly sins—envy, lust, covetousness, sloth, gluttony, wrath, and pride—those motivations that are the hidden principles of modern and postmodern sociopsychology.

Beauty is nondeterministic (though not by any means disordered). It carries a necessary element of pure surprise, but the surprise is followed by a realization of the appropriateness, the necessity, even the inevitability of the surprising element. Laurie Anderson's electronic augmentations of her voice are beautiful, and surprising, but also, like a good story, quite inevitable once one has heard them. It is the right next move, into a human voice or song that could vibrate whole planets, that could shear crystals into their pure faces by their subsonic rumble, the easy piercing of their supernatural soprano. Likewise the beauty of the skating rink at the Galleria Mall in North Dallas, this airy cool surprise under the arched tinted glass vault five stories high, a tiny figure skater turning lightly in the air as she completes her twist, the soft hubbub of voices from the cafés and restaurants. A coarse middle-class beauty, perhaps, but one that Manet would have surely painted if he were there.

Beauty is always paradoxical. It is not mere chaos and nonlinearity but the paradoxical coexistence of chaos with order, nonlinear discontinuity with linear flow and predictable repetition. Artists who make chaotic works of art are deceived by their own laziness of vision and ignorance of science into thinking that the world as it is, is ordered and linear, and thus that the artist's work is to add an element of the random. But nature, society, even middle-class life, are already full of surprises, and the addition of randomness without countervailing order is a relaxation into a sort of miserable expectation. The theorem of Pythagoras is beautiful neither because of the linearity of its logic and its diagram nor because of the loony and disordered surds—the square roots—that it plays with and cancels out on the way; but because of their coexistence in the same proof. In pi we find both the unitary perfection of the circle—merely an inflated point—and the tormented chaos of its nonrepeating decimal expansion. In the golden section ratio 1: 1.618 . . . there is the same paradox, between its irrational decimal expression and the logical simplicity of the Fibonacci series that generates it, between the open-endedness of the Fibonacci spiral and the visual closure of the five-pointed star, which contains the golden section in its proportions.

Beauty always opens up a new space, as it were, at an angle to the old—sometimes at ninety degrees, perpendicular to the old, so that it casts no projective shadow upon the old coordinates and has no more dimension in those terms than does a point. That new space is also a new time, so that we find we must invent such terms as *eternity* to describe it. But it always has a source in the old and is continuous with it. In the final minutes of *King Lear* we definitively break through, not once but two or three times, into new whole dimensions of feeling and insight. We think we can hardly breathe in that strange new world, but we find we can, like the dreamer who sometimes, in the terror of a drowning dream, takes a panicked breath and finds that it draws as sweetly and nourishingly as real air.

Though beauty can exist within violent and energetic processes, it always has its own poise and elegance; it is not needy but overflowingly plentiful, not tilted or drawn toward some area of lack or absence. We meet this quality of violence and energy proceeding from fullness rather than lack especially in music, in the urgent wildness of the strings as they ride over and around the *Dies Irae* in Mozart's *Requiem,* or the eerie shrieks of Bulgarian and Macedonian tribal songs. In the art of their representation, the terror of death and the anguish of sexual desire are the sign not of absence but presence, not of lack but plenitude.

Nevertheless beauty always exists at some border or terminus of the world. Though it has no lack in itself, its natural place is at the edge of the great lack, the great precipice of the world, where past being abuts upon what is not, not yet. Consider a Mayan blood-ritual stela: a princess, depicted in a fanatically detailed low relief, is undergoing her self-laceration. She is at the edge of the world. Dressed in her exquisite and brutal panoply, where representation cannot be easily distinguished from representation of representation, she draws in spasms a thorned thread through her tongue. Out of her falling blood effuse monstrous visions of her ancestors. It is horrifying but unmistakably beautiful; in a strange sense it is not tendentious, its eyes are open in a tragic and mystical joy.

Lack, tendentiousness, absence would draw a work of art back into the world, where it must go to fill its appetite and slake its need. The beautiful can exist at the edge precisely because it has nothing to lose and everything to give away. It expands by its own plenteousness into the void and makes new presence there. Nor is it finally rejecting the past—to do so would be to evince another kind of lack. Its whole substance is the past; it is in solidarity with being and is being's own amateurish leap into a new space and time.

It is this very plenitude of presence that arouses the resentment of those who cannot feel beauty and who know (and deny) that they are shut out from the feast of being. Shakespeare's Iago cannot bear the spectacle of the daily beauty in Othello's life. He must discredit it to gain his peace, even though he knows that the need to discredit it proves conclusively that it is real; he must therefore conceal from himself his true motivations and replace them with political and psychosexual ones.

One of the most powerful metaphors of beauty is indeed sex and reproduction. The most beautiful expressions of plants and animals are their flowers, their mating plumage, their mating rituals. But for those who have experienced beauty most deeply, sexual attraction, that motivational trigger-structure designed to stimulate behavior leading to the perpetuation of the species, is only a metaphor for beauty, a precursor of it. Even among the animals there seems to be a playfulness and at the same time a more-than-utilitarian grace in their sexual games. The male grackle with the finest harem is not a mere master of signals, but a stylist.

Beauty, we feel, has much to do with the senses and might even, on a fresh spring day, appear simply the exercise of the capacity of perception, how good it is to be alive. I have seen a

Ghanaian gold pendant, a fat coiled mudfish heavy with detail, its grotesque splay head of greasy orange gold set with little sightless piggy eyes, its finned backbone and plump flanks crimped into a tight whorl, just as one might dig it out of the dried mud of a watercourse, still alive in the drought, happily subsisting on its own reserve of slime. But the work of art celebrates not only the life of the fish but its miraculous survival into another life. It both arouses the appetite to broil and eat the good thick flesh and denies it, for the flesh is strangely excrementitious, to eat it would be coprophagy, and on the level of representation it is made of incorruptible and indigestible gold. We might say that beauty is like eating, but that it is more like sex than eating, because sex requires the postponement of eating and even the death of the individual to promote the survival of a new generation; but then we must say that it is even more like the hope itself, the mystical giving away, which is the secret heart of sex: for the new individual will not be the same as its parent, the new life not a clone of the old.

Even when the beauty is a coarse and sensual one, like that of the splendid steamed clams in ginger and garlic that Tong's, our local Chinese restaurant, serves every day, there is still something of the supersensual about it too. Somehow that fine cook manages to keep the benthic pungent bitterness of the raw clam, its thin stony shell, its coarse feathery beard, the hint of its alien briny existence, though all civilized by the green onions and the hot sweet ginger sauce. It reminds us of the realm of the drowned as it heartily nourishes our life.

There is always in beauty a global quality, a reference to the whole world and to its further meaning. We find this especially in beautiful scientific ideas, like the Gibbs free energy formula, $G = U - TS + pV$. G is the work-power of any system, its thermodynamic potential, even if the system is the whole universe. We obtain it by the simplest and most elegant means: from U, the internal energy of the system (locked up in its atomic and molecular binding and kinetic energies, etc.), we subtract its temperature (T) multiplied by its disorder or entropy (S), and then add its pressure (p) multiplied by its volume (V). And that's it. We find the global quality likewise in the theory of evolution by natural selection, where the iterated feedback of variation, selection, and heredity can produce all the exquisite forms of life (and perhaps, with sheer molecular endurance substituted for heredity, all the forms of chemical and physical existence). That universality is also to be found in the self-reinforcing logic of tragedy, in the symmetry of the markings of a Siamese cat, in the branched forms of coral, in the unerring curves of Haida totem poles, even, mysteriously, in the earthy, oaken, flowery bouquet of a great wine. Somehow all of these beautiful things, when appreciated as beautiful, obscurely remind us of the whole universe, its special flavor, its interface with what is not (yet).

Beauty is what makes life worth living. It is like those moments when we acknowledge our own shame and break through into the anguished tears of recognition, the joy of full presence. I have seen a dark slow look of love pass over my wife's face gazing at her invalid mother, who was as unconscious of her daughter's regard as my wife was of mine. In that glance was all the recognition of her mother's sacrifices, her past as a young mother passing on what she had to her children, her limitations, her illness, her future death, her failings and dogged spirit. My wife bit her lip and turned away and made a casual remark in a rough tone. Painful and embarrassing as the moment was, it was very beautiful and had in it a strong rush of the imagined joy of paradise. Such things make life full and dense.

And sometimes beauty simply celebrates itself, like the dragonfly in Miklós Radnóti's poem "June":

> Behold the noon in its miraculous power:
> above, the flawless and unwrinkled sky;
> along the roads, acacias in flower;
> the stream throws out a comb of golden ply,
> and in the brilliance, bold calligraphy
> is idly, glitteringly, written by
> a boastful, diamond-budded dragonfly.
> (*Foamy Sky: The Major Poems of Miklós Radnóti*)

It is not hard to cite examples of beauty, though they somehow have a tendency to elude analysis and lapse into cliché or vagueness; they need the life of poetry to match and catch their own. It is much harder to say what is not beautiful. The ugly, beautifully described, can be beautiful; the describable has integrating principles and a sufficient wealth of detail to be described, and is thus already beautiful. It would be tempting to say that the ugly is the indescribable; but this is too elegant. After all, there is much that is indescribable about beauty, and the divine itself is traditionally both indescribable and beautiful. Perhaps the very quibble over describability, this very process of unwieldy qualifications and reservations, is ugly; the word *describable,* used often enough, begins to take on a miserable and tedious meaninglessness. If the author, now, were trying barrenly to show off by means of a display of complex reflexiveness, as for instance in some works of deconstructive critical theory, we might begin to approach the full-blown nastiness of the truly ugly, and thus our author should have done us the favor of presenting us with a pure sample of an important quality, that is, ugliness itself, for our analysis.

Perhaps the difference between the indescribably beautiful and the indescribably ugly is that the former is both simple and infinitely deep, whereas the latter is superficially complex, too incoherent for description, but limited. I can remember as a child the pleasure of tictacktoe and the miserable ugliness of the discovery that the game was limited and that there was an automatic drawing strategy. The beautiful—the game as it first appeared, a simple set of rules generating an infinite play of strategy—had turned into the ugly, a superficial complexity concealing a wretched automatism.

We experience this quality sometimes in committee meetings, especially where an elaboration of due process disguises the struggle of political faction, which in turn disguises the voracious and cruel neediness of personal interest. Dioramas in museums can have that nightmarish claustrophobic quality—imagine being trapped in one, scrabbling at the plaster veldt and the dead tufts of grass, with only the stuffed ostriches and forever paralyzed glass-eyed antelopes for company. And yet a diorama can also be charming, magical, evocative, dreamlike; and a stage set will often rely on the explicit limitedness of its space and means for its pathos and mystery. And even political committees can under the right circumstances be beautiful—consider the noble beauty of the *Federalist Papers*.

The indescribably beautiful is always, I believe, partially describable because higher hierarchical levels contain and reference lower ones, and lower ones are infused with meaning by their higher context; whereas the indescribably ugly is indescribable because it has no clear hierarchical structure by which the part can synecdochically stand for the whole. But this distinction is unbeautifully simple, for the ugly can sometimes be ugly precisely because of the patness and completeness of its hierarchical structure, and the beautiful often, as in a Brahms concerto, subtly but luminously undermines its own order.

Let us refine the distinction and thus redeem the ugliness of these qualifications and exceptions. A hierarchy that is too neat and complete subverts the very need for hierarchy, which is to unify disparate material, to preserve the surprise of difference precisely by holding it within a frame of unity, rather than dissipating it by separation from what might provide a contrast. If there are no surprises or differences there is no need for hierarchy and the intelligibility it brings with it. Hierarchy is in this case merely a muddying elaboration of an identity relation into one of subordination, like a subordinate clause that adds no meaning to the sentence, déjà vu all over again. (But Casey Stengel, the author of this last phrase, like Yogi Berra of "It's not over till it's over," is beautifully funny precisely because he turns the redundancy into a delightful parody of itself, and uses an apparent syllogism as a trope to convey a necessary intensification.) The false hierarchy of an ugly thing muddies its reality, which is boringly simple; the tangled but true hierarchy of a beautiful thing is always clear, intelligible, and revelatory of mysteries otherwise left obscure.

This last formulation, which identifies ugliness with both needless elaboration and with falsity, gives us a good handle on the ugliness of shoddy stylish commodities that give the consumer less, while promising more, than they pay for; and it highlights the hypocritical lie, the lie by one who has not warned us he is lying, as close to the heart of ugliness. The lies of a publicity agent, a politician, a used car salesman, even an advertiser (as long as they are not disguised, say, as a government announcement to disabled veterans about the availability of insurance), are not particularly ugly, because nobody expects the truth from such figures. We are not offended by an actor's false claim to be Hamlet or Lear. However, lies by public moralists, academic social critics, self-styled defenders of the public's right to know, and tribunes of all kinds, are always ugly; and especially ugly is their pretended scandal at the lies of ordinary rascals in government and business.

Something with a single function may not be very beautiful, but it is not ugly in itself. As we have seen, naked power struggles are not necessarily ugly; only when they are cloaked in the falsifying hierarchy of due process do they become obscene. But there is even another twist to ugliness: oversimplification is as ugly as overelaboration. When the struggle is over and one side dominates the other, or even when one side has got the moral high ground of the other, the collapse of difference into identity is ugly. One of the ugliest things there is must be the claim that what is in fact a necessary and beautiful hierarchy, containing and preserving differences and surprises without denaturing them, is merely a cloak for power relations, when that claim comes either from the mere malignity of the insensitive or from the strategic rhetoric of those who themselves seek coercive power. Any kind of reductiveness that eliminates genuine higher- or lower-level qualities, as biological, cultural, economic, and social determinism did in the human sciences, and as racial and gender politics are doing in the humanities, is ugly. It is ugly both to hierarchize the truly undifferentiated, and to level the truly hierarchical.

Coercive power in general is ugly, as opposed to true hierarchy, which is the only human defense against coercive power; because power tends to subsume the controlled into the controller and thus to eliminate surprises and to diminish the complexity of the hierarchy. Hierarchy can only exist if all its members have a semiautonomous identity, maintained by vertical level-distinctions and the horizontal individuality-distinctions they guarantee and maintain. Hierarchy disappears with the advent of power relations, which collapse lower levels into higher ones or which, by attempting to dissolve the higher levels, collapse them into the lower. And when hierarchy disappears, so does difference and the autonomy that comes from difference. The only real difference is significant difference, as any shopper in a supermarket knows well; and differences that are not held within a hierarchical matrix that gives them meaning are no differences at all. Democracy is misconstrued as a way to get rid of hierarchy; instead it is an attempt to create true hierarchy, a flexible and porous one in which the relations of subordination and superordination are guaranteed by consent rather than by power. As the Framers of the United States Constitution knew, when democracy turns into an attempt to destroy hierarchy, it destroys autonomy, consent, and permitted difference, and instead of democracy we get bureaucracy or the tyranny of the majority.

Let us attempt to sum up the ugly, then, as any decay or reduction of a deeper beauty into a shallower one. A deep beauty has many hierarchical levels and needs them to articulate and maintain the differences of its elements. A pretentious ugliness is one that possesses more hierarchical levels than are necessary, and thus it displays the structure of a deeper beauty but not its substance of differences; a reductive ugliness is one that possesses fewer levels than necessary, so that the genuine differences belonging to a deeper beauty are lost and destroyed (or deconstructed). The falsity that is essential to ugliness is precisely the disjunction between the form and substance of hierarchical depth.

This is why death—not seen as the boundary and shape of a life, but death as the negation of life, death as the process of decay and corruption, death as a moral solvent, death as feared—is one of our paradigms of ugliness. Death is the literal reduction of higher levels of organization and value to lower ones. Death is a great lie, a false disclosure of the "real" nature of life. Death says that this is all life is, really. From this point of view we can now see the error of those who, in an attempt to avoid what they feel to be an arrogant human hierarchy of values, refuse to recognize any distinction between higher and lower forms of life, and especially between human beings and other animals. With the best of intentions they participate in the ugly and vulgar lie of death, and by denying the greater value of a human being over a maggot, a bacterium, a virus, are philosophically guilty of murder.

Yet death seen in the other sense, as the boundary and formal edge in time of a life, is one of the most beautiful things we know. We make room by our death for other lives, for a sharing of the world with them, and an enrichment of the world by the multi-leveled structure of our relations with them. The further articulation and elaboration of any organism, even if justified by its own internal richness of difference and need for distinctions, must be balanced against the requirements of the larger systems of which that organism is a part. A greater depth of beauty in the whole system may require the limitation, even through death, of any part of it. The only human cell that is immortal is a cancer cell; all others give up their lives for the good of the whole body, or if they are germ cells, give up the integrity of their genetic structure in the great chaos of sexual recombination.

It remains for us, in this phenomenological exploration of the feel of beauty, to distinguish it from other experiences that, though related to it and consistent with it and not its opposite as ugliness is, should nevertheless not be confused with it. The experience of beauty is clearly a pleasure, a very powerful if also an extremely intangible and fugitive one. But it is not reducible to other pleasures, and has a clear and distinct quality of its own.

As we concluded in our discussion of Tong's clams, there was a special quality, a poetry, that raised them above being simply good to eat. A rich and delicious perfume may or may not be beautiful as well as sweet-smelling; if it is blended with a certain complexity and subtlety, so as to be suggestive of some larger meaning—if its sweetness is cut by some hint of the sages of New Mexico or the saffron of Macao or seaside rooms in Nauplia, or if it expresses the strange element of the girl-child and the old dame in every mature woman, then it can be beautiful as well as sweet. But even a merely sweet perfume can be beautiful smelled in a room redolent of woodsmoke and pine needles, or recognized as that of a person one used to know. Beauty is not reducible to the pang of sexual pleasure in the loin, in the marrow of the shank and pelvis, or in the thickness of the breast and pit of the stomach; though that pang can be part of a beautiful moment, combined with the pathos of your lover's dream as he or she tells it to you.

Beauty is closely related to but not the same as other transcendent experiences: the glory or despairing triumph of heroic action; oceanic religious ecstasy or trance; the deep intellectual satisfaction of scientific or philosophical or mathematical insight; the rapture of love; the irresistible upwelling of laughter at absurdity or comedy. Though these are not the same as it, each need turn only a degree or so to become the beauty experience. What each needs is a tang of the intangible, a suggestiveness, a fleetingness because it connects with the utterly unexperienced, a gratuitousness or supererogatoriness. Beauty is to those other experiences as mercy is to justice.

Beauty is not, either, the merely sublime. The sublime can be impressive, and can satisfy our rage and envy and covetousness when we compare our own wretched inner selves with the grand generosity of the world as it is, and our pride at our separation from it. Jean-François Lyotard admirably expresses these feelings in his essay "What Is Postmodernism?" where he argues against beauty and in favor of the sublime. We artists sometimes miss beauty and plump for the sublime instead, out of lust and sloth, lust for perversion and sloth in the face of the subtle demandingness of the muse. The rich will sometimes buy the sublime, the historically interesting, rather than the beautiful, again because of sloth—the sublime hits you immediately between the eyes, the beautiful is more shy and retiring—and because of their gluttony for new things, the greed of the connoisseur. The sublime goes beyond the world's edge at the expense of the world rather than as a gift to it.

Nevertheless, there is a trace of the sublime in all beauty, even the common beauties of elegance and prettiness. It is the itch of the world to explore, to go beyond where it has reached already. But beauty, even when it ventures over the hills and far away, wears its mother's party dress.

Likewise, some modernists and postmodernists have preferred the grotesque to the beautiful, as being more "honest" to the horrifying realities of eating, death, reproduction, political control, and desire. Again there is a hint of the grotesque in much beauty, and there can be much beauty in the frankly grotesque. The richest hierarchies of beautiful form contain a thousand paradoxes and heterarchies and ambiguities, each helping to generate new dimensions of hierarchy at ninety degrees to the old ones. Beauty—to anticipate a later argument—is the creative principle of the universe, and is thus in part a transgressive force. But the grotesque pursued as a program, as an ideological stance, produces only ugliness; it is a rejoicing at the breakdown of hierarchical structure rather than an interesting and enriching tangle in it.

The purpose of this opening chapter has been to set the experience of beauty squarely before us and to distinguish it from what it is not. But we have so far only a set of impressionistic descriptions of it and of its foils. The purpose of this book is to develop a coherent theory of beauty, one that understands its inner dynamic and not just its outer appearance. We will need to venture into the many realms of science, anthropology, philosophy, and even mathematics to find out how beauty works.

The contentions of this book are that beauty is not marginal and unimportant, not merely subjective, not an effect of something else such as social power or libido, and not idiosyncratic to the individual. Instead, it is central to all meaningful human life and achievement, it gives access to the objective reality of the universe, it is an independent and powerful experience in its own right, and it is culturally universal both in its general characteristics and in many details. Its absence in the family, in schools, and in public life is a direct cause of the worst of our social problems and a contributing cause of all others, and its restoration to the center of our culture will bring real improvements to the lives of all citizens.

But before we go on to develop a theory of beauty, we need to examine why, and how, beauty was rejected, withered, and died as a central cultural goal in the last two hundred years.

Two

Shame, Modernity, and the Death of Beauty

T HE IMAGE of beauty with which the previous chapter began, of the girl in her mother's dress, implies a sophisticated observer of her and a curious feeling of shame—shame at the memory of one's own first step into the role of adulthood, shame at the gaucheness of one's humanity. The very euphemism *aesthetics* bears witness to an anguished sense of disloyalty against our first vulnerable feeling of wonder at the world. In this chapter we shall take up three themes: shame, the triumph of modern consciousness, and the idea of the political left—the gauche—and its corollary, the political right—*le droit*. Using these ideas we will explore the decay of beauty as an ideal and as a technical enterprise in the last two centuries.

The work of three thinkers—a literary theorist, James Hans, a sociologist, Thomas Scheff, and a professional mediator, Suzanne Retzinger—has established shame as the hidden cause of much contemporary cultural damage. Hans, expanding on the work of René Girard, admirably identifies religion, with its sacrificial underpinnings, as an attempt to incorporate the shame of our physical existence into a cultural vessel that can contain it. He does not, however, speculate on the possible connection of the decline of traditional rituals with our contemporary problems with shame, and instead enjoins on us a kind of existentialist enjoyment of life in which shame is not institutionalized. Scheff and Retzinger, building on the work of Helen Lewis, identify unacknowledged shame, which they explain as being the natural result of a real or imagined exclusion from a desired social solidarity, as a major source of personal dysfunction and barren social conflict. They distinguish two pathological reactions to shaming situations: overt undifferentiated shame and what they call bypassed shame. The signs of the overt type are a cycle of shame at one's own shame, rage at oneself, rage at the person who has shamed one, shame at one's own rage, and so on. The subject is flushed, inarticulate, trapped in painful emotion, and crippled in function. Bypassed shame, in contrast, is recognizable by a sudden sharp pang of shame followed immediately by a total suppression of it, covered up by glib and rapid speech, ingenious but superficial and flawed thought, a paralysis of the emotions, and a capacity for affectless and conscienceless cruelty.

This chapter will perforce be a painful and awkward one, arousing feelings both of discomfort and anger in the reader. Both Scheff and Hans point out that shame itself, even more than shameful objects and actions, is the object of massive euphemism, repression, and denial. We deny that we feel shame, because shame is a shameful feeling to have. We would much rather feel an ennobling guilt, which we have safely internalized where nobody can see it.

From this point of view such works as Goethe's *The Sorrows of Young Werther* (admirably analyzed by Scheff), Flaubert's *Madame Bovary,* and Joyce's *Dubliners,* especially "The Dead," can be seen as the attempts by genius to grapple with and transform into beauty a peculiarly virulent modern strain of our most ancient human curse, shame itself. In *Werther* a social shame that the hero cannot acknowledge is repressed into romanticism; in *Madame Bovary* the country girl in her mother's dress finds that the only way she can tear that gauche garment from her body is by death; in *The Dead* the sexual and political provincial transforms shame into epiphany.

Modern writers at the height of their genius are able to achieve a painful and provisional standoff with the shame of life. Perhaps the task would be easier in a traditional society, where sophisticated mechanisms have been developed over millennia to deal with the pain and extract from it the strange epiphanic renewal of beauty that it contains.

If we look at the foundation myths of any culture we will find some deeply shameful act at the origin of the human world. Take, for instance, the Eskimo story of Sedna and her father Anguta. Sedna marries a dog against her father's wishes; the father kills her dog-husband; on the way back a storm rises and Anguta, to lighten the boat, throws his daughter overboard; she clings to the boat and he, to get rid of her, cuts off her fingers. Or the Shinto story of how the sun-goddess Amaterasu was shamed by her bad brother Susa-no-wo, who threw a flayed horse through the roof of her weaving-hall. Her subsequent retirement to a cave deprived the world of sunlight—as did the shamed rage of Ceres in the myth of Persephone. Or consider the biblical story of the Fall, of the shame of Adam and Eve at their disobedience, their lies, and their nakedness; or the shameful story of Kronus castrating his father Uranus with a sickle, and the generally incestuous provenance of the Greek gods; or the shameful murder of the corn god in Amerindian mythology; or the various shameful acts of tabu murder and incest in Australian aboriginal creation myths.

These myths express the essential knot of our human predica-ment. The threads of that knot include: the problematic coexis-tence of a reflective mind with a smelly, sexed, and partly autono-mous body, the horror of death, the ambiguous relationship of human beings with the rest of nature, the incestuous paradoxes of kinship and parenthood, the capacity to lie given us by language, and the difficulty, obligation, and anxiety inherent in the socio-economic acts of gift-giving and dividing the fruits of the hunt. Our aboriginal human philosophy tended, with the natural econ-omy of dualism, to divide the cultural from the natural. Today, in the light of evolutionary biology and cosmological science, we may be in a position to revise that ancient dichotomy. We recognize that to some extent other species share those reflexive paradoxes, and that our version of them is only an intensification—across certain crucial thresholds—of tensions inherent in the evolutionary process itself and belonging perhaps to the feedback nature of the universe as a whole. However, even if we do replace an absolute division between the human and the natural with a more continuous evolutionary gradient of increasing reflexivity, and even when we come to recognize nature as not just what is given but as the very process of accelerating evolution that transforms the given, we must still deal with a world in which greater and lesser levels of self-reference, feedback, intention, and freedom must somehow coexist.

And this coexistence is essentially shameful. We are ashamed about our sexuality, about how we came into the world, about how we did not at one time exist, either as a species or individually. We are thus ashamed of our parents, especially when adolescence forces on us a constant attention to the process of reproduction that originated us; and the reflexive appetite of the mind makes us at the same time seek out the nakedness of father Noah, the nakedness of mother Jocasta. We are ashamed at our bodies, which display an impure and inextricable mixture, a mutual *adulteration,* of the intentional and the instinctive. We are ashamed about eating, because, whatever we eat, we are assuming, upon the confessedly untrustworthy warrant of our own biased judgment, that we must be more valuable than what we destroy with our teeth and digestive juices. Hence we naturally find the end products of eating to be objects of disgust. We are at the top of the food chain and feel an anguished and unrepayable obligation to those beings that gave up their lives for us.

We are ashamed about our economic system, whereby we define ourselves as members in good standing of our community, and thus as human beings; we are never quite sure whether we have given the right gift, or given a gift when we should not have, or not given a gift when we should; and we are shamefully anxious about whether we have been given the right gift. We are ashamed at what we have made, whether because of uncertainty about its worthiness or because of the obligation we incurred to those parts of the world we destroyed to make our new contribution to it. The institution of money, by which we extend through time and space the reckoning-up of the balance of obligation for past gifts and so transcend the limitations of memory, is a basically shameful object of contemplation; we call lucre filthy and are always seeking ways to delegitimize our own economy, at least as it applies to ourselves. We are, finally, ashamed at our own feelings of shame, our own reflexiveness, our awareness of our awareness.

However, as James Hans points out, it is precisely in this whole area of experience—the reflective interaction at the deepest level with nature, with our origins, with our means of life, with our closest kin, with our community as an object of obligation, and with our very self-consciousness itself—that we encounter the beautiful. Thus in ways that are bearable to us because their story nature insulates us from their direct personal application without denaturing their meaning, our myths conduct us into the realms of shame where the hot blush of consciousness—the "Blank misgivings of a creature / Moving about in worlds not realized," as Wordsworth put it—can be transformed into the delicious shiver of beauty. The severed fingers of Sedna become the beautiful warm-blooded marine mammals by which the Eskimos survive; the sun-goddess Amaterasu is lured forth from her cave by the newly invented mysteries of dance, comedy, and the mirror of self-awareness; Adam and Eve get knowledge as well as death, and give birth to history and to human redemption; the genitals of Kronus arise from the sea-foam as the beautiful goddess of love; the corn god's golden hair waves in the wind as the silk of the ripening maize; and the pratfalls and transgressive gaucheries of the aboriginal tricksters are the source of all human arts and graces.

Shame and beauty, then, share a common root. The work of such myths is both to show us how to experience the beauty we have paid for with our shame and to remind us that if we attempt to avoid or repress the shame, we will find ourselves as cut off from beauty as the world was from sunlight in the myths of Amaterasu and Persephone. Why beauty and shame should be so closely connected is a matter of considerable interest, which we will take up at a later point. Suffice it to say now that both involve the emergent and aroused reflexivity, self-reference, and feedback of nature, both within and beyond the sphere of human culture.

Many of the major institutions of traditional societies—ritual in general (especially sacrifice, but also funerals, initiations, birthing ceremonies, puberty rituals, and purifications); religious codes of behavior; customs of modesty in clothes and deportment; courtship and marriage; hereditary privilege; etiquettes of education; the traditional forms of the arts—may be seen in this light as other ways of ensuring a productive passage through shame to beauty.

Sacrifice transforms a shameful act—the public killing of a living being or its substitute—through collective acknowledgment of our condition and recognition of the nature of the universe into an experience of beauty. Other rituals similarly accept, frame, organize, and elaborate the chaotic shame inherent in death, life-crisis, birth, sexual awakening, and pollution in such a way that we recognize the beauty that also attends those moments of embarrassing emergence and self-reference. Religious moral codes give us clear boundaries to transgress and ways of seeking beautiful repentance when we do transgress. Modesty, by explicitly concealing our animal nature, draws attention to it; the blush brings out the special conscious beauty of the face. Courtship and marriage accept and concentrate the shame of sexuality, and thus allow its strange mutually mirroring beauty, the lovely pathos of its nakedness, to be revealed.

Hereditary privilege thematizes and renders acceptable the shame of inequality, whether that inequality stems from lucky genetic differences of talent or from the luck of the social circumstances of birth and upbringing; our shame at the relative paucity of our achievements is accepted as integral to the beauty of service to what is nobler than we. The necessary and institutionalized inequality of parent and child during the child's minority is the source of both humiliation and the most exquisite tenderness. The traditional relationship of teacher and student—one of the few other examples of explicit and prescribed personal inequality that remain in the modern world—transforms what is potentially the most murderously shameful situation of all, one person telling another what to think, into a beautiful and mutual pursuit of the truth. (Perhaps, ironically, it is a misplaced bad conscience about this inequality that makes the contemporary academy so furious a scourge of hierarchy and domination; who in a democracy are more oppressed than the students of a politically correct professor?)

The traditional forms of the arts are also, in a less immediately obvious way, both reminders of our shame and revealers of beauty. As we shall see later, the traditional panhuman artistic genres are keyed to our neurophysiological makeup in such a way as to remind us of our materiality, our mortality, the automatism of our delight, as well as the strange reflexivity of our awareness. We are embarrassed by our pleasure in rhyme, by the sweetness of melody, by stories with neat endings, by gorgeous color combinations, and by the great natural genre of representation in general. It is in and through this very corniness, this shameful twinge of natural response, that the mysterious powers of beauty take flesh and reality. But many have felt that the beauty was not worth the concomitant twinge of shame. The aesthetic severity of the modernist has its precedents: in the Hebrew prophets and the Islamic mullahs with their shame-denying injunctions against representation, in the Athenian feminists who in their destructive fury castrated the statues of the gods, in the Byzantine iconoclasts, in the followers of Savonarola who burned the Botticellis, and in those of the puritan John Knox who forbade the beauties of church decoration and ritual and who smashed the stained glass and abolished the old church music.

We are now, perhaps, at a point where we can start to explain the title of this chapter and answer the implied questions with which it began: In what sense did beauty die in the last two hundred years, why did it die, and what can be done to bring it to life again?

It is a truism of sociology that modernity was the period during which, for a multitude of reasons—greater personal mobility, the contraction of the unit of production from the extended family to the individual worker, the drive toward political liberty, the spread of literacy, urbanization, and so on—many of the traditional institutions of preindustrial society fell into decline. Myth, ritual (especially sacrificial ritual), religion, traditional customs of modesty, courtship, marriage and family, hereditary privilege, and the traditional art forms all lost their hold upon the allegiance and imagination of the people.

Modernity can also be usefully defined as that period in which politics came to be polarized into left and right. Thomas Carlyle, writing about the French Revolution, was the first writer we know of in the English language to use the term *left* in its political sense, in 1837 (though *gauche* and *droite* had been in political use in France since before the turn of the century). By 1887 the left-right distinction was a regular and recognizable description of the two wings of the British parliament. It has been precisely since politics divided itself into left and right that beauty began to be rejected by artists and critics, or euphemized and denatured as aesthetics. Are these events connected? How, in other words, may we relate these three interesting facts: the function of traditional institutions in accepting shame and thus releasing its mysterious twin, beauty; the decline of those institutions in the nineteenth and twentieth centuries; and the rise of the left and the right? Let us examine briefly the psychology of the political right and left, for if we consider beauty deeply we will find that it cannot endure their presence, that the beautiful and the left-right political dyad are mutually exclusive. Other kinds of political affiliation, such as tribal, civic, national, or even factional loyalties (as in Dante's Florence), seem to be able to coexist with beauty, and politics was regarded both by the Greeks and by the Framers of the United States Constitution as an activity of beautiful excellence; it is not politics in itself that is fatal to beauty but some particular characteristic of it that has emerged in the modern world.

Let us begin with the right. As the old ritual institutions faded and lost their legitimating and unifying power, those who, through natural talent, inherited wealth, or the effects of the last generation of hereditary privilege, had been left in favorable or leading positions in society, found themselves at an impasse. The shame of their position—their knowledge of their kinship with the beggar, the cripple, the idiot—was no longer rendered acceptable by the old institutions. The political right arose out of a new response to that shame: outright denial of that shameful kinship with the less fortunate. If we turn to the right we deny the discomfort of shame altogether and impose upon ourselves the rectitude and adroitness of the political right, which exports to the Other both its own gaucheness and its own sinisterness. Keeping up that rectitude is exhausting, and one unconsciously resents the effort. Hence the cruelty of the right. All the shame of one's own condition is projected upon the poor, the racially other, the female, the unfortunate, the left, the left outside. Once one's own disgrace has been displaced and shifted to the margins, its stink becomes associated with the Other and is the justification of an unthinking contempt.

In extreme economic conditions when it appears that the privileges of the in-group are being eroded, as in the period of hyperinflation that preceded the rise to power of the Nazis, that contempt can turn to hysterical hatred. It is highly significant that the Nazi pathology arose in the atmosphere of shameful defeat fostered by the Versailles treaty, in which the Germans had to bend the knee to the French, whom they despised; and that it seemed to them that the Jews were the beneficiaries of the disruptive economic conditions created by the treaty. As Scheff points out, Hitler's formula of the "stab in the back" is a masterful use of rhetoric to mobilize repressed shame. Instead of sacrifice, which implicates the sacrificer in the shame of existence, the Nazis instituted the Holocaust, which was an attempt to annihilate the source of shame. The Holocaust, as a name for these events, is thus both chillingly accurate and profoundly misleading.

Many human qualities—solidarity, hatred, dogged loyalty—can be aroused and manipulated by such means. But not beauty. Nazi ideology was accompanied by gigantic and sentimental attempts to recreate the beauties of traditional public rituals and public arts. But the torchlight parades, the monumental architecture, the *völkisch* paintings of wholesome Aryans reaping the fields, all ring hollow and do not capture the shock and mystery of beauty. The reason is that shame has been denied, not accepted and incorporated. In contrast, the operas of Wagner are beautiful precisely because, whatever Wagner's views, the shame of life cannot be alienated from his heroes and heroines and comes home tragically to roost.

The Nazi pathology is an unusual and extreme transformation of the right, with many left-wing elements, such as hatred for and envy of the rich (displaced to the Jews) thrown in. The normal attitude of the right to their Others is not one of hatred, but of a comfortable and easygoing condescension, even affection. The self-righteousness of the right is implicit in the very word itself. Right is correct, unblemished, unshamed, preserving of face; it is the *Recht,* the *droit,* the dextrous, the dutiful, the adroit. It is one's due, one's right, one's proper fate, one's portion, one's appointed moira, or fate, or slice of life. The fugitive and elusive quality of beauty avoids the right in normal circumstances not so much because of its potential for brutality but because of its breezy philistinism, its complacency, its apparent incapacity for shame.

Beauty equally avoids the left, and for the same reason: its denial of shame. But the mechanism of denial is very different from that of the right, and more interesting. In a society where, because of the breakdown of traditional institutions, one's fate is largely in one's own hands, and there exists no ritual or sacrificial means of catharsis, personal failure becomes unbearable. This is why social unrest occurs, paradoxically, not in conditions of extreme and established social inequality, but during periods when that inequality has already lost its legitimacy and efficacy. One can no longer explain the dissatisfactions of one's life—and thus dissolve them— by reminding oneself of one's proper station in society; one has no proper station.

Shame, fundamentally, does not come from a lack of ability to *have,* or *possess;* it comes from the consciousness of a lack of ability to *give.* The shame one feels at being excluded from the communion of the "right" people—not getting a share of the hunter's prey, or getting a share different from what one expects—derives basically from a suspicion that our own gift to society was not acceptable and thus that our exclusion from the human exchange system may, shamefully, be justified. It is the shame of Cain. (Here I must acknowledge my debt to the brilliant classical scholar Edwin Watkins, who has done so much to unravel the meaning of sacrifice and of the hero's moira, his fate, his slice of the divided kill.) Among our close relatives, the baboons, such shame can lead to massive changes in the balance of the brain chemicals, overstress, sexual dysfunction, and collapse of the immune system.

The real horror of the condition of the underclass, it might be added, is not the lack of possessions, but the inability to give gifts. (It is well known that the poor are proportionately more generous than the rich; it is their attempt to rejoin the human exchange system.) The sting of this inability is *exacerbated* in a free and equal society, not assuaged; and this is why underclasses as such are only found in such societies. An exploited proletariat or peasantry at least has something to give, something to exploit; its problem is not the shame of incapacity to give but the lesser shame of being unable to defend its interests. The only way to alleviate the condition of the underclass, then, would paradoxically be to allow it to give to the rest of society, not take from it.

Money is the measure of other people's collective obligation to us; and someone else's money is our obligation to them. If there is too great a disparity between my money and somebody else's, then I feel the shame of an unpayable debt, which, if I am a leftist, I deny by attacking the legitimacy of the economic system itself. But to see how a leftist gets to this kind of maneuver we need to understand the basic emotional transactions of his or her ideology.

The first move of leftist ideology is to repress and bypass the unbearable shame of personal failure, real or imagined, and transform it into pity for the oppressed. Feelings of sadistic rage and icy noble justice, which one could not legitimately feel on one's own behalf, as a bad loser, one can indulge without limit on behalf of someone else—or something else, in the case of animal rights extremists. Nothing is as pleasant as an emotion normally forbidden as wicked that is justified by the wholesome and righteous glow of altruism.

The second move of the leftist pathology, then, is to translate pity for the oppressed, via the natural human sacrificial-scapegoat instinct, into hatred for the rich and successful: hence class war and the institution of the Gulag. This hatred is essential and central to the leftist ideology; it is not the product, as rightist hatred is, of extreme and paradoxical circumstances, but is the very heart and soul of the position, its fundamental psychological payoff and the sure sign of its presence. True pity for the poor and the unfortunate—which is a real, and most beautiful human emotion—accepts its own shame and extends to all creatures rich and poor, and makes itself felt by immediate, unpublicized, and local attempts to ameliorate the condition of others; it is incompatible with hatred. We can tell ideological pity from true pity by the killing.

Once the killing starts, another feedback mechanism springs into being; our shame at our crimes is denied, and transformed into further hatred, which must be slaked by further crime, leading to further denied and redirected shame. This is the essential mechanism of the phenomenon of the Terror.

Envy, too, which is one of the immediate offshoots of shame, plays an important part in this move. Leftists are no more immune to the temptations of luxurious living than, say, TV evangelists (in fact they are often, when they get into power, sybarites and sensualists of amazing ingenuity and scope, as we may see from the lifestyles of folk like Chiang Ching and the Ceauşescus, not to mention people closer to home). But the shame of the desire for goods whose very value derives from those whom we believe have shamed us, a desire for them *because* those goods belong to those who have shamed us—our reluctance to admit the mimetic desire that makes us value what they have made valuable—leads us to project upon the rich a monstrous greed and insatiable appetite that is in fact our own, the fevered product of our imagined deprivation. The established rich are often rather bored with expensive and complicated possessions that require time-consuming upkeep and protection, and sometimes lead lives of remarkable simplicity. The true gifts of wealth are empty space and empty time. It is the nouveaux riches who conspicuously consume, who displace the shame of their earlier poverty upon the Other; we might define the leftist as an unsuccessful member of the nouveaux riches. If the leftist does achieve success and wealth, the paradox of his or her position is itself a shame that must be denied, with a new access of sectarian cruelty.

In recent years there have been further developments in the leftist denial of shame. One of them is liberal guilt, which is a way of turning shame inward, into a self-punishment (rather than accepting it and turning it outward into creative action). Another is the current demonization of the human race itself as the despoiler of Nature: the very word *pollution* bears witness to the primitive roots of our shame and to an unconscious thirst for purification rituals that we no longer possess. Another current development of the same kind is working itself out in the anguished debates of some extreme feminists about how best to deny the inherent shame of our division into two sexes—deny the distinction itself, or deny the moral legitimacy of the male sex.

Many of the fundamental shame mechanisms of the left are, as with the right, implicit in the name, *left*. We have already glanced at the gaucheness, the anguished feeling of social shame that we at first deny, then transvalue, and finally even flaunt as the banner of our political correctness, the gauche transformed into the political left. The left is also the left out, the excluded from social communion; and it is the sinister, both in the imagination of the right and, romanticized, in its own. The left hand is the one used in many traditional societies to wipe one's behind; it is the *linkisch,* the clumsy, the dark, the "female," the maladroit hand. But in the leftist ideology all these weaknesses are gloried in, transformed into the victim's anguished defiance, and fastened upon the enemy as the consequences of his crime.

What happens to beauty in the world of leftist ideology? The fundamental move was the replacement of the beautiful with the aesthetic—a word that came into English from Germany just seven years before the first known use of *left* in its political sense. Thus the sweet old shame of beauty could be erased in the severe and intellectual pursuit of aesthetic purity. The aesthetic carries with it a large vocabulary of technical terms whose possession protects the elect from any embarrassment. Once the aesthetic was detached from its humanity, its shame, and its mystery, it could then be turned to political uses, and political correctness—paradoxically, "rightness"—became the fundamental principle of leftist aesthetics. Today the only defensible principle—the only undeconstructable idea—in poststructuralist criticism is power. The essential relation that the concept of power implies is one-way, unambiguous cause and effect. Instead of the work of art finding its own free way to existence, mysteriously taking up and combining its influences into its own reflexive feedback system, it became an epiphenomenon of its political origin.

Another move, which countered the shame of the involuntary, the organic, the genetically imprinted in the beauty experience, was to insist on the originality of the artist, the artist's heroic will and defiance of the natural. In an apparently opposite move, leftist modernist art would sometimes emphasize the physical and sexual, but in a context in which moral judgments were ridiculed, and always in a way calculated to shock and pain the bourgeois onlooker, to leave the viewer alienated and disgusted with all the slime, as it were, of the artist's imagination now amusingly fastened to him or her rather than to the artist, who as the arranger of this little trick remains untouched by it. Yet another move is a willful obscurity in the arts, calculated to induce a feeling of shame in the audience, reader, or viewer—nicely caught in Bob Dylan's lyric: "You *know* something's happening here, but you don't know what it is, / Do you, Mr. Jones?" The shame of the disadvantaged social misfit (who didn't understand opera, perhaps) is turned back with a vengeance upon the wretched middle-class rube, who now becomes the victim in turn. And here we have the driving force of the avant-garde.

Another leftist aesthetic move was quickly suppressed in countries with leftist governments, but left, so to speak, to flourish in the bourgeois democracies: the abandonment, on strict rational principles, of all rationality in art. Such work was designed to subvert the hierarchical power system of the right—it was, as it were, deliberately *wrong!*—but again it was a kind of attempt to mirror back to an imagined oppressor the shame, and thus confusion, of the oppressed; or by breaking down all distinctions to bury in a general chaos the painful difference between shame and justified complacency. Postmodern criticism, detecting shame, personalized as the transcendent signifier, even in the ideas of author, self, reader, meaning, text and world, has proceeded to feed them one by one to its flames.

It may well appear in this welter of aesthetic theory—I have barely scratched the surface—that there is no coherent leftist position in the arts. But this is not quite true. One way of characterizing the common themes of leftist aesthetics is to say that whereas the right denatured beauty in the direction of the merely pretty, the left did so in the direction of the merely sublime. Perhaps, moreover, the very variety of impressive theories is an example of one of the fundamental characteristics of bypassed shame—the swift glib verbalization, the affectless ratiocination that covers up the wound, that skins and films the ulcerous place.

I have dwelt at greater length upon the peccadilloes of the left than on those of the right, but this was partly because the former are more interesting and less thoroughly investigated by others. If the leftist reader—I doubt if this book will have many rightist ones—should attempt to escape the shame of recognition of his or her own motivations by dismissing its author as a conservative or cryptorightist ideologue, I shall quite understand. But such a reader should know that I accuse myself of many of those very leftist dishonesties; if I describe them, it is because I have experienced them, and it is to my own shame if others have not made the same mistakes. Perhaps I am biased by my own need for exorcism. Certainly I have felt, both as a youth and as an adult, the dull glow of resentment at art that seemed to take pleasure in my incomprehension, or in my miserable and helpless sense that something I held dear had been unjustly and gleefully misrepresented. But it is the purpose of this book to accept and pass through the shame to the beauty that lies within it.

Other processes, which I have described elsewhere as characteristic of modernism in general, also contributed to the death of beauty. One was the mistaken idea, inherited from Enlightenment physics, that the world was an unfree and linear deterministic mechanism, and thus that creativity and freedom could only exist in a supernatural sphere, or, if there were no such sphere, that only the random, the gratuitous, and the fauve could escape the tyranny of matter. (As we shall see later, the rest of the physical world is only less free and creative than we; nothing is more natural than freedom and creativity.) Another process was the increasing assimilation of artistic activity to the metaphor of industrial production as the combustion of organic fuels. Art became the fire of burning traditions. Another process was demographic: a huge wave of adolescents, the result of improved hygiene and lowered infant mortality, temporarily swamped the other generations in most nineteenth-century industrial countries, leaving behind an ideal of artistic originality modeled on male adolescent ideas of freedom: hypercritical, sexually demanding, aggressive, and egocentric.

But fundamentally it was the left-right dyad that killed beauty, by denying its shame. To adapt a saying of Brecht's, there can be no tragedy either in a leftist or a rightist world. In this time when that dyad seems to be losing its force and disappearing, we may begin to hope for a rebirth not only of tragedy—accepted shame—but also of beauty.

Three

The Biology of Beauty

THE TITLE of this chapter in itself represents a wholesale questioning of much of the modernist and postmodernist consensus. In order that we shall be quite clear about the extent of the investment—and the painful divestment—that I believe is necessary if beauty is to be brought back to life, it might be helpful to summarize that consensus as it concerns beauty, and to sketch in advance, before they are argued, the main assertions that this book asks the reader to consider.

Most modernist and postmodernist thinkers today would largely agree with the following propositions.

1. Human beings have no nature.
2. Nature itself is passive before our constructions of it.
3. There is no essence or meaning in things.
4. There is no hierarchy in things other than what is imported into them by our power-seeking constructions of them.
5. These is no progress. (Modernism began with a triumphant belief in progress; its contemporary heirs, however, have largely abandoned it.)
6. The past is irrelevant except as a record of mistakes and abuses.

To these we made add two more specifically aesthetic propositions.

7. Beauty is not a reality but a social construction.

8. (As we have seen:) The aesthetic consists in the absence of shame.

Finally, four main substitutes for beauty have been offered in the realm of aesthetics, held sometimes together and sometimes in opposition to each other.

7a. The function of the aesthetic is novelty. Deconstruction is the heat-death or final perfected state of this view.

7b. The function of the aesthetic is subjective expressiveness (the interpretation of personal experience in terms of the latest and most prestigious popular psychological theory).

7c. The function of the aesthetic is to demonstrate politically correct attitudes.

7d. The function of the aesthetic is to demonstrate the absence (Derrida) or presence (Heidegger) of Being in the world, Being conceived of as essentially prior to reflection, culture, and the linguistic construction of the world.

To these propositions we may oppose the essential assumptions of this book.

1. There is a real human nature.

2. There is a real universal nature, partly knowable by appropriate means, including us but not completely determined by our constructions of it.

3. There is an essence and meaning in things.

4. There exist real hierarchical properties in the world, which involve scaling, the organization of living and nonliving systems, and levels of reflexivity and sensitivity.

5. There is such a thing as real progress.

6. Any significant work in the present must include and be the culmination of the past.

From these assumptions follow the theses of this book:

7. Beauty is a fundamental reality.

8. Beauty exists only in the accepted presence of shame.

7a. Beauty, though it may be surprising, must also be familiar; it connects past and future, the known and the unknown.

7b. Beauty is culturally universal and goes beyond the subjective self and beyond inner desire; it is a true description of the real world.

7c. Beauty is the guide of politics, as it is the core of morality and speculative understanding; it is not the handmaiden of politics.

7d. Beauty is the defining property of Being, but only if Being is conceived of as complicated, interfered-with, reflexive, epistemological, and at least potentially aware in its very essence.

These assumptions and propositions are not an attempt to set the clock back. The modernist and postmodernist positions were in many ways an intellectually honorable and often brilliant attempt to solve a number of major philosophical and social problems that had been bequeathed to them by the Enlightenment and by the history of Europe in general. These problems included: the Cartesian division of the world into mind and matter; the apparent linear determinism of physical nature; the logical, moral, and psychological problems generated by the dogma of a transcendent, immaterial, single, omniscient, and omnipotent deity; a growing unease at the irresponsibility of metaphysics; the experience of multiple frames of reference and their apparent irreconcilability; the existence of alienating modes of production, unjust social hierarchies, and class distinctions; and the increasingly questionable assumption of Western racial and cultural superiority.

Thus any revision we made in the postmodern consensus, even in the noble cause of beauty, must also include a satisfactory answer to those problems that the consensus was designed to address. I believe that such a revision is possible, on the basis of the new set of conditions that is now emerging as we approach the end of the second millennium.

Contemporary brain science, which embraces fields as far apart as psychology, neuroanatomy, paleoanthropology, ethology, artificial intelligence, genetics, and neurochemistry, simply has no use for the mind-matter distinction; the mind-body problem is not a problem any more. Nature turns out to be only partly linear and deterministic; much of the time it is nonlinear, self-organizing, unpredictable, reflexive, and stable only through its own feedback processes.

New theologies propose an immanent, emerging deity or deities, learning their own nature through the experience of the evolution of the universe and especially through our own participation in their existence. Metaphysics in the traditional sense, which sought to find some discussable realm for those entities and qualities—the soul, freedom, meaning, etc.—which we felt sure were real but could find no place for in the physical world, is no longer necessary, for the physical world now makes generous room for those entities, indeed demands their emergence as new physical features of it. Physical science now includes metaphysics. A whole theory of the interaction of different frames of reference, known as evolutionary epistemology or dramatistics, has arisen; there is no need for a desperate relativism or a defeatist pluralism, and any discourse that can indicate the incommensurability of different frames has already transcended it.

In the emerging technology, any work that is inhumanly repetitive and alienating can be mechanized, leaving the creative and interesting tasks for human beings. Economics is in the process of a profound transformation, as economic value ceases to be based on labor and scarcity, and becomes a warmer, more flexible measure of creativity and density of information. The collapse of the socialist states has shown us the folly of attempting to eliminate hierarchy; we got instead the dictatorship of the *apparat*. Democracy is now appearing in its true light, as a way of insuring that the necessary hierarchies we rightly construct and fill with personnel are flexible, just, and accessible to anyone with the talent and desire. The increasing liquidity of all forms of value is dissolving the old class systems. The West, having lost its former assumptions of superiority, finds that it can take pride in being the first (and the most advanced) in the recognition of the value of other cultures; meanwhile in a number of fields a natural classicism is emerging, panhuman and culturally universal, to replace the old partial and exclusive Eurocentric classicism.

This new view of the world perhaps sounds optimistic; indeed it might be objected, in the light of the previous chapter, that it could turn into another attempt to eliminate or at least deny our shame. On the contrary; I believe that it will remove the obstacles to our recognition of our shame, and restore to us the most fundamental and most fertile shame of all, the conscious recognition of ourselves as creatures of matter, animals that feel and think as we eat, breed, and die.

Perhaps the finest description of living matter as revealed by the science of biology can be found in Thomas Mann's *Magic Mountain*. It remains as true today in its broad outlines as when it was written a lifetime ago.

What was life? No one knew. It was undoubtedly aware of itself, so soon as it was life; but it did not know what it was. Consciousness, as exhibited by susceptibility to stimulus, was undoubtedly, to a certain degree, present in the lowest, most undeveloped stages of life; it was impossible to fix the first appearance of conscious processes at any point in the history of the individual or the race; impossible to make consciousness contingent upon, say, the presence of a nervous system. The lowest animal forms had no nervous systems, still less a cerebrum; yet no one would venture to deny them the capacity for responding to stimuli. One could suspend life; not merely particular sense-organs, not only nervous reactions, but life itself. One could temporarily suspend the irritability to sensation of every form of living matter in the plant as well as in the animal kingdom;

one could narcotize ova and spermatozoa with chloroform, chloral hydrate, or morphine. Consciousness, then, was simply a function of matter organized into life; a function that in higher manifestations turned upon its avatar and became an effort to explore and explain the phenomenon it displayed—a hopeful-hopeless project of life to achieve self-knowledge. . . .

What then was life? It was warmth, the warmth generated by a form-preserving instability, a fever of matter, which accompanied the process of ceaseless decay and repair of albumen molecules that were too impossibly complicated, too impossibly ingenious in structure. It was the existence of the actually impossible-to-exist, of a half-sweet, half-painful balancing, or scarcely balancing, in this restricted and feverish process of decay and renewal, upon the point of existence. It was not matter and it was not spirit, but something between the two, a phenomenon conveyed by matter, like the rainbow on the waterfall, and like the flame. Yet why not material—it was sentient to the point of desire and disgust, the shamelessness of matter become sensible of itself, the incontinent form of being. It was a secret and ardent stirring in the frozen chastity of the universal; it was a stolen and voluptuous impurity of sucking and secreting; an exhalation of carbonic acid gas and material impurities of mysterious origin and composition. It was a pullulation, an unfolding, a form-building (made possible by the overbalancing of its instability, yet controlled by the laws of growth inherent within it), of something brewed out of water, albumen, salt and fats, which was called flesh, and which became form, beauty, a lofty image, and yet all the time the essence of sensuality and desire. (Thomas Mann, *The Magic Mountain*, pp. 274–76)

The discovery of the structure of DNA and the function of RNA and our first groping steps to synthesize new forms of life have not invalidated any of Mann's supremely wise and visionary conception. If anything he does not go far enough; the notion of the physical inorganic universe—that "frozen chastity of the universal"—which he inherited from the nineteenth century, was still essentially the deterministic, linear, and mechanistic one of Newton, Maupertuis, and Laplace. In the last few decades we have seen Mann's description of life as an incontinent, mysterious, self-reflective and self-organizing feedback system extended by nonlinear chaos theory, fractal mathematics, and Prigoginian dissipative systems theory, to every level of material being, including the inorganic.

Mann calls life "shameless," and what he means is extremely complex: made capable, by its self-consciousness, of shame, and helplessly revealing the shameful characteristics of sensuality and desire; yet accepting that shame as the price of its privileged existence, and thus, to an observer, blushing defiant of its proper modesty. This shameful-shameless beauty and reflexivity have now been found, in a dimmer and simpler form to be sure, in the turbulence of liquids and gases, in phase-changes such as crystallization and partial melting, even in the processes by which the elementary particles and before them the four forces of physics precipitated out of the incandescence of the Big Bang.

This is not to say that there is nothing linear, predictable, and mechanistic in the universe—nothing pure and chaste. Each level of being might regard the lower and earlier levels rightly as more innocent than itself. If there were no unself-conscious, honest, and straightforward objects in the world there would be no standard by which to judge the proper degree of modesty (that is being violated, acknowledged, and reaffirmed). In fact the anguished shame—and beauty—of the world come not only from self-reflection itself, but from the turbulent and densely enfolded region of *contrast* between the relatively self-reflective and the relatively unreflective. What is most painfully and delightfully reflected upon is, after all, always the previously unreflected. Certainly there never was an unalloyed purity in the universe; the cosmos hides its privates with a fig leaf, and, if the cosmos is the body of God, then God, coyly, hides his—or hers—too. The blush, which Darwin saw as one of the defining characteristics of humanity, is the very condition of physical existence, and there is no way back to a time before the blush. The blush is time itself.

But that world-blush is also the beauty of the world (each new moment of which is forever young, we might say, but wearing its mother's dress). Many of the higher animals have, through the feedback process of evolution, added a new twist to this reflexive spiral or helix and have developed a capacity to recognize that beauty in certain limited forms. The colors and shapes of the flowers are a precise record of what bees find attractive, and it would be a paradoxically anthropocentric mistake to assume that, because bees are more primitive organisms—as they indeed are— there is nothing in common between our pleasure in flowers and theirs. The play behavior of many higher species has an irreducible element of pleasure in beauty, a rejoicing in their sheer physical capacities—flight, in the case of the jackdaws that Konrad Lorenz so lovingly observed, or speed and power, as among frolicking horses, or agility and coordination, among cats. Animal communications often seem to be as much for the sake of beauty as for use, as Charles Hartshorne observed in the antiphonal music of tropical songbirds, or has been recently remarked in the complex individual songs of the humpback whale.

Most salient of all is the strong element of beauty in animal rituals, especially mating rituals. It is important to look closely at how such rituals function and evolve, because their implications for our own rituals are very interesting. Generally when a survival behavior can be accomplished easily, without contradicting other instinctive behaviors, it is done automatically and without fuss and fanfare: breathing, perspiring, sleeping, and waking up. We do not notice such behaviors as "drives"; they are more part of what an animal is than what it is driven to do. When two behaviors contradict each other, however, a space between them is sometimes formed that does not belong strictly to either. The animal now must use its nervous system to the utmost; you can see a squirrel or sparrow thinking when its natural and uncomplicated fear of humans is contradicted by its natural and uncomplicated desire for the crust of bread you have put out for it.

When the two contradictory behaviors are both social, their intersection can become the stage for the most elaborate and beautiful displays, dances, songs, even dramas (as when in the triumph ceremony of the greylag geese, that Lorenz describes, the heroic lover attacks an imaginary counterfactual enemy goose as a sign of its exclusive devotion to the beloved). In mating ritual reproductive behavior is contradicted by territorial or intraspecific aggressive behavior. An area between them is opened up in which the linearity of an uncontradicted system will no longer work, and elaborate, nonlinear, highly self-reflexive and mutually reflexive feedback processes take over. Here the linear mathematics of continuous functions no longer applies, and the mathematics of catastrophic and fractal discontinuity comes into its own.

When this immediate individual-to-individual feedback system is in turn supplemented by the much larger and slower feedback system of evolution, remarkable changes and developments can take place in a species as a whole. Mating rituals directly affect the reproductive success of an individual: thus an individual with better ritual pigmentation, better plumage, better-looking reproductive organs, better songs and dances, or better antlers with which to stage the gladiatorial games of sexual rivalry, will end up with more progeny; and so the genes for those qualities can rapidly pervade the gene pool of the species, crowding out the others. Hence the beautiful feathers of the peacock, with their fractal designs that attract predators no less than mates; the neon displays of tropical fishes; and the extraordinary artistic activities of the blue satin bowerbird, whose courtship involves the building of an elaborate and useless bower, its decoration with colored objects, and even its painting with the juice of berries. Hence also the development of the elaborate tribal structure and status hierarchy of our close relatives the baboons, chimpanzees, and gorillas. The guenon monkeys have differentiated themselves into dozens of microspecies purely, it would seem, on the basis of their body-decoration.

More ominously, as a result of this feedback, some species have developed ritual behaviors and the structures required for them, to such an extent that their very survival is threatened: the giant elk is thought to have disappeared because the antlers of the male, used for ritual combat, were too large and heavy for its body. It is commonplace for individual animals to sacrifice their lives for the opportunity to mate; anyone who has seen the tragic and gorgeous spawning run of the chinook salmon, in their brilliant and terrifying nuptial-funeral colors, recognizes the kinship with our own bittersweet dramas of passion. Humankind is not the only species that does not live for bread alone and that can risk all for love.

The realm of life groans with the contradictions of sexual reproduction. Most unsettling of all, sexual reproduction comes in a package which includes programmed individual death. Sex was itself a response to the very theme of life, which is acceleration in the ecological transformation of the world; we must remember that most of the remarkable developments of the higher species of life occurred in the last couple of hundred million years, and that for over three billion years before that, life changed very much more slowly. However, even those slow changes, and the alterations in the ecology that they brought about, would have begun to overload the adaptive capacities of asexually-reproducing (self-cloning) organisms. Sex was a biological innovation whose survival value was to increase the extent and speed of adaptation to natural change. Without sex, the enormous recent acceleration in the rate of evolutionary change could not have occurred. However, for sex to work—for there to be room for those sexually produced, monstrous, infantile, and protean organisms that might be the progenitors of new species—it required its dark twin, programmed death. An asexually-reproducing organism is relatively immortal—that is, it takes an external force or deprivation to kill it—but in a sexually-reproducing organism a cell which turned off its own death program would be a cancer cell.

Going even further back, the appearance of life itself might be interpreted as a response to apparently irreconcilable contradictions inherent in matter. (Here I must acknowledge deep debts to J. T.

Fraser and the International Society for the Study of Time.) When matter condensed out of energy, it bought a long and stable endurance at the cost of abandoning the uncommitted and flexible quantum indeterminacy of its radiant substance. The trouble with energy is that left to itself it flies off radially from itself at the speed of light and dissipates itself according to the inverse square law; and by thus blowing up its own envelope of space-time, which it carries with it everywhere, it flattens out the very curvature of space-time from which it got its being and intensity in the first place. If this was survival, survival was pretty trivial—an unbearable lightness of being.

Matter was more sober. It stayed in one place and took a part in the local history of the universe, recording and reacting to local events, collapsing the indeterminacy of incident bundles of energy into definite events and work, affecting other bodies, and thus confirming its own existence and that of its neighbors. It could act. It took on, like mortgages, many new forms of linear determinism, expressed in the laws of physics and chemistry. But the forms of matter, though enduring, did not possess the immortality of energy; they could be shattered or melted and could not repair themselves, except in the very limited way in which crystals can reform themselves out of a melt along the same planes and angles. Life solved this problem by means of its power to replicate itself; and thus the form or pattern of life could survive its material substrate, as a sonnet survives in its copying from an old book destined for the flames to a new printing. And in solving this problem it took on all the quivering ambivalence that Thomas Mann describes; each new solution to the contradictions of existence raises new contradictions. These contradictions are in fact the general and original forms of which shame is perhaps the latest and most elaborated, most explicitly reflexive development. But these contradictions are also the spurs to the emergence of new and more exquisite forms; and beauty is our word for that emergence.

Before we go on to discuss human ritualization, a final, even more speculative note on the history and evolution of the universe seems called for, upon which a group of philosophers including

Koen de Pryck, Alexander Argyros, Karel Boullart, and I have been working. We believe that the pattern I have described, of the emergence of a whole new level of existence out of a contradiction or insoluble paradox in the previous, more primitive level—and then the discovery that the new level of existence itself contains its own peculiar tragic problems—resembles for good reason the concentric nested pattern of transcendent logics generated by Gödel's incompleteness theorem.

Gödel proved that for any system of mathematics or logic there would be a permissible proposition of the form of "This statement is not provable," whose truth or falsehood could not be proved within the axiomatic resources of the system itself. There may be a larger system that can decide its truth or falsehood—we, for instance, can easily see that the proposition is both true and unprovable—but such a system would in turn contain paradoxes unsolvable in its own terms. Roger Penrose, in his excellent book *The Emperor's New Mind,* points out elegantly that a Turing machine— that is, the perfect linear calculator—must, in order to give a complete answer to a problem, be able to tell itself to stop. Problems of the Gödel's paradox type are such that a Turing machine can never stop, once it is engaged in their calculation. In order to make it stop, there must be a level jump—as when we get tired of calculating pi to another ten thousand decimal places, and turn off the Cray, or, more subtly, when we recognize that a mathematical series is converging toward a limit, discontinue the calculation of the series, and either obtain the limit by other means or use the limit to whatever decimal place we choose to round it off.

Perhaps the physical universe itself emerged as the new level in which the solution to problems inherent in a primal mathematics might be found—perhaps the world is the only solution of a logical paradox. Perhaps space and time emerged as ways to keep contradictory propositions "artificially" apart, where they could not interfere with each other. We will look at some of these issues in chapter nine.

Are we like Turing machines ourselves, then, with some appalling proposition waiting for us, in whose attempted solution we will be unable to turn ourselves off? Or can we contemplate the mandala of being, its concentric circles of more and fundamental contradictions, and so transcend the system itself? Are we always able to recognize that the calculation is converging toward a limit, or an attractor, and thus free ourselves from that final trap? Is not death, inquires Karel Boullart, the Belgian philosopher, simply our arrival as an organism at such a problem?

And is not shame, perhaps, the anguish that we feel when we recognize that there may be a point of view in whose eyes we ourselves are as trapped and helpless as a lower organism, as the living flesh of which our bodily substrate is made, as the wretched Turing machine that goes into the paralysis of not being able to turn itself off? Might we not be in some other mind's gaze a comic automaton, another lower organism whose true being is revealed in the cheap and vulgar rictus, as David Lindsay put it, of death? And is not the shame of sexual nakedness precisely its reminder of the ancient double bind, of the Gödelian paradox itself, that we cannot account for our own existence?

Consider the human body, and its remarkable differences from the bodies of other mammals. One of the most obvious is our nakedness; we stand hairless but for odd tufts here and there emphasizing such body parts as the head and face and the genitals. All other land mammals of our size, and all of our relatives the primates, including all tropical primates, are covered with hair. Some much larger tropical species, like elephants and rhinoceroses, are, indeed, also hairless; the reason is that their greater size implies a higher ratio of body volume to body surface, and a larger and more stable thermal reservoir; and thus they do not need hair. Human beings, however, are pantropic in their habit—they live in all climates—and are much smaller; without clothing and shelter they would be at a massive disadvantage.

We, like the other animals, evolved; and it is a truism of evolutionary logic that if a given bodily structure (such as hair) is not necessary, and cannot be adapted to another purpose, those individuals that possess it will be at a disadvantage, if only because of the metabolic drain on their resources that the structure's production and upkeep requires. This disadvantage will tend statistically to result in fewer such individuals surviving to reproduce, a thinning out of the genes for that structure in the population, and a preferential rate of increase for genes not specifying that structure. The same applies in reverse; if a species would be better off with hair, say, to maintain a constant body temperature, hair will be selected for. As we have seen in the case of the peacock's tail and the elk's antlers, however, sexual ritual can contradict this biological law.

The most plausible explanation for our nakedness, then, is that it is the result of sexual selection in ritual courtship, and that we developed clothing originally both for ritual body decoration and also to replace for thermal purposes the hair that we had lost. The invention of clothes, a by-product of our ritual, enabled us to survive even in cool temperate and arctic climates; and so as hair was no longer necessary for survival, it never came back. Thus our nakedness is a result of our early culture.

And here we see a new principle of reflexive feedback enter the, already tangled, iterative, and turbulent process of natural evolution. Cultural evolution—that is, a process of change in behavior that can happen in a single generation and be passed down through imitation and learning to the next—now takes a hand in biological evolution, in that iterated cycle of sexually or mutatively generated variation, selection through the preferential survival of useful traits in the population, and genetic inheritance. Biological evolution takes millennia; cultural evolution takes years. Yet the culture of a species, especially in its effect on sexual and reproductive success, is a powerful determinant of which individuals survive to reproduce. The faster process of change—culture—will drive and guide the slower one—biology.

Many of the other peculiar characteristics of the human body can be explained in the same way: its upright stance, its long infancy, its developed vocal chords and otolaryngeal system, its extraordinary longevity (especially in the female), its relative early menopause, its relative lack of specialized armaments—big teeth and claws, and so on—its opposable thumbs, its superbly refined and coordinated fine motor system, its continuous sexual readiness (most animals are in heat only for a few days in the year), its huge brain.

The upright stance reveals the full beauty of human primary and secondary sexual organs to each other; it enables hunters and gatherers to carry meat and vegetables home, and therefore to have to remember who gets which share; thus it also helps us to have a home to carry things home to, and thus a ritually charged place and a kinship system that can serve as a set of rules for distribution; and it enables parents to carry babies in their arms who are helpless because they require a much longer infancy period than the young of other species, a long infancy demanded by the need to program children in the complexities of the tribal ritual. The upright stance also changed the normal mating position from mounting to face-to-face, thus encouraging that extraordinary mutual gaze that is the delight of lovers and the fundamental warrant of the equality of the sexes: an equality that was absolutely essential if the human traits of intelligence, communication, and imagination were to be preferred and thus reinforced.

Our ritual songs, improved every year, demanded complex voice-production systems that could also come in useful for communication in the hunt and other cooperative enterprises. Our long old age enabled the elders—especially the postmenopausal wise-women—to pass on the ritual lore and wisdom. Our lack of bodily armament was compensated for by the development of weapons, which could be wielded by thumbed hands liberated by our upright stance and controlled by an advanced fine motor system— thumbed hands required to enact the ritual actions and paint on the ritual body paint and carry the ritual objects and make the ritual clothing and gather the seeds and roots for our tribal kin. Sexuality was extended and intensified relatively to other animals and was adapted from its original reproductive function into the raw material of an elaborate ritual drama that pervaded all aspects of society.

And the great brain mushroomed out, transforming its substructures to the new uses and demands that were being placed on it, pushing out the skull, diminishing the jaws, wiring itself more and more finely into the face, hands, and speech organs, specializing particular areas of the right and left to handle new linguistic, musical, and pictorial-representational tasks, developing a huge frontal lobe to coordinate everything else and to reflect upon itself and its body and its death, and connecting that higher-level reflective consciousness by massive nerve bundles to the limbic emotional centers—thus creating a unity of function between the intellectual and the passionate which is close to the heart of our deepest shame and which has thus been denied by most of our recent philosophical systems.

From this point of view personal physical beauty takes on a new importance. Breeders of dogs and horses can tell by very subtle physical signs, in the carriage of the head, the set of the eye, the delicacy of proportion, whether the animal is likely to possess psychological characteristics such as intelligence, heart, and concentration. The intangible elements of human beauty—beyond those obviously related to reproductive and survival success, such as big breasts and hips, clear skin, broad shoulders, straight legs—are evidently such external bodily signs of internal neural sophistication. Those intangible elements that we refer to when we say that someone has beautiful eyes or a beautiful expression or that we are captured by in someone's way of moving—the things that make us watch a great film star—can be quite different from conventional beauty. They can quickly overwhelm any deficiency in the brute appeal of the hunk, the nice piece of ass, beefcake or cheesecake. The lovely ambiguity in the word *grace*—divine favor, and excellence in physical coordination—wonderfully catches this other quality; though in the context of the darker price of human excellence it is significant that grace is also a purifying blessing (from Old English "blissian," to wound or make bleed) before meals. When we fall in love, and thus mate and have offspring, we do so often because we are captured by such qualities. Thus we look the way we look as a species largely because that was the way our ancestors thought intelligent, strong, loving, and imaginative—ritual-ready—animals ought to look. We are the monument to our progenitors' taste.

Many of our creation myths show an intuitive grasp of the strange process by which the cultural tail came to wag the biological dog. The story of the clothing of Adam and Eve, where (the awareness of) nakedness is the result of shame, which is in turn the result of self-knowledge, expresses one aspect of it. Again in Genesis the punishment of Eve for her acquisition of knowledge, that she must suffer in childbirth, nicely expresses the fact that one of the parameters of a big-brained viviparous species like ourselves is the capacity of the female pelvis to allow the passage of a large skull. Hence also the beauty for the male of the female's wide hips and the motion they make when walking. The big (and to the male, attractive) breasts of the human female, and her dependency upon a protecting male during lactation—also referred to in Genesis—are likewise the sign of a nurturing power that can deal with a long infant dependency, and thus produce human beings of intelligence, wisdom, and aesthetic subtlety. Babies without protecting fathers must enter adulthood earlier, and cannot be fully instructed in the tribal ritual; they thus need smaller brains, and smaller-hipped and -breasted mothers to bear them.

Our deep feelings of embarrassment and anger at these facts, the flush that rises to our faces when we think of our own biology, are the signs of that shame which we would deny but whose acceptance is the only gate to beauty. That beauty is summed up in the great pictorial genre of the madonna and child. At present this tragic contradiction makes itself felt in our society by a conflict between female roles—of a nurturing that produces the best and noblest and most loving human intelligence and of the very exercise of that intelligence. The means and the end of nurturance are thus perceived as opposed in our society. But we should not deceive ourselves that if this problem were solved, the solution itself would not produce its own contradictions even more tragic and shameful, and even more potentially beautiful.

One persistent theme of creation myths all over the world is the presence of a trickster, who somehow transforms the forces of nature so that they assist rather than hinder the cultural program. The story of how Odysseus tricks Polyphemus, the caveman, into rolling away the rock-door of his cave is one survival of such a myth. South American Jaguar tales, in which fire is adapted to human use, have the same gist. We find in these myths both the shame of our mistreatment of our mother, nature, and the nostalgia for the beautiful arcadian landscape that we like to imagine as having preexisted the birth of self-consciousness. Polyphemus lives on the slopes of Etna, by the vale of Enna where the fountain of Arethusa rises, mingled with the waters of her pursuer, the arcadian river-god Alpheus; where Proserpina wandered before her rape by Dis; the loveliest arcadian landscape of all, the closest to the volcano and the source of fire, painted by Bellini and sung of in Handel's *Acis and Galatea*.

If the human ritual as we have envisaged it was to have its original evolutionary function, it must have involved a dark and terrible element. For if some members of the tribe enjoyed greater reproductive success, others must have enjoyed less. If some were selected as preferred mates for their intelligence, wit, loving nature, prudence, magnanimity, honesty, courage, depth, sanguine disposition, foresight, empathy, physical health, beauty, grace, and strength; others—the dullards, whiners, liars, blowhards, hoarders, spendthrifts, thieves, cheats, and weaklings—must be rejected. The most brutal throwbacks—the rapists, those who grabbed the food and did not share it, those who could not follow the subtle turns of the ritual and internalize the values that it invented and implied—would be cast out from the tribal cave, into the outer darkness, where there is wailing and gnashing of teeth. Defective infants would be abandoned on the mountainside; adults polluted by impiety, crime, incest, madness, disease, or their own exercise of witchcraft would be led to the borders of the village lands and expelled. Oedipus, who was exposed though not defective at birth, is among other things a symbol of our guilt at such rejection: when he does return, as all buried shames must, he pollutes the city with his unconscious incest. The Old English monster Grendel, that wanderer of the borderlands, the descendant of Cain, is another type of such outcasts, and the image of the scapegoat.

But indeed, the fragile virtues of the human race would have been impossible without this terrible and most shameful selection process. If we consider how morally imperfect we are as it is and how the best and most recent research shows that moral traits are to a considerable extent inherited, it may be a grim satisfaction to reflect how much worse we would be if we had not selected ourselves for love and goodness. Abraham's willingness to sacrifice his son Isaac at the command of the Lord (whom we may take, for mythic purposes, to be the evolutionary imperative of the human species, the strange attractor drawing it into being) is necessary, paradoxically, to bring about a more loving and juster humanity. We had better be worth the price.

Indeed, our moral growth has, more recently, caused us to recoil in revulsion from those ancient practices; but that growth was partly their result. And the process has not ceased, and we had better face up to the fact. Every time a woman chooses a man to be her husband and the father of her children, for any good personal reason—for his gentleness and his wit, his confident strength, and his decent humility—she is selecting against some other man less noble in character, and either helping to condemn him to the nonentity of childlessness or to be the parent, with some less morally perceptive woman, of children who are likely to inherit their parents' disadvantages. It is horribly cruel and shameful, if we think about it, but I believe there is a strange and terrible beauty to the magnitude of the mating choice that is at the root of the troubled exaltation we sometimes feel at a good wedding.

The rituals of sacrifice, and their later and more subtle developments as tragedy or eucharist, are the human way of rendering this ancient horror into beauty. Sacrifice has a peculiar element, which we might call "commutation": every sacrifice commemorates a previous sacrifice in which some much more terrible act of bloody violence or costly loss was required. Abraham is allowed to sacrifice a ram instead of his son, who was due to the Lord; the Greeks can burn the fat and bones and hide of the bull to the gods and eat the flesh themselves. Instead of a whole firstborn son, only a shred of flesh from the foreskin need be given. When the process has been going for a long time, the sacrificed object can become apparently rather trivial. Cucumbers are sacrificed in some African tribal societies; Catholics and Buddhists burn candles; almost all Christians break bread. Thus every sacrifice is an act of impurity that pays for a prior act of greater impurity, but pays for it at an advantage, that is, without its participants having to suffer the full consequences incurred by its predecessor. The punishment is commuted in a process that strangely combines and finesses the deep contradiction between justice and mercy.

The process of commutation also has much in common with the processes of metaphorization, symbolization, even reference or meaning itself. The Christian eucharistic sacrifice of bread not only *stands in* for the sacrifice of Christ (which in turn stands in for the death of the whole human race); it also *means,* and in sacramental theology *is,* the death of Christ. The Greek tragic drama both referred to, and was a portion of, the sacrificial rites of Dionysus— both a use and a mention, as the logicians say, or both a metaphor and a synecdoche, in the language of the rhetorician. The word *commutation* nicely combines these senses: in general use it means any substitution or exchange, as when money in one currency is changed into another, or into small change, or when payment in one form is permitted to be made in another; in alchemy it can be almost synonymous with transmutation, as of one metal into another; in criminal jurisprudence it refers to the reasoned lightening of a just punishment to one which is less severe, but which is juridically taken as equivalent to it; in electrical engineering it is the reversal of a current or its transformation between direct and alternating current; in mathematical logic it refers to the equivalency of a given operation, such as A multiplied by B, to its reverse, B multiplied by A.

Shakespeare's *The Merchant of Venice* is a profound meditation on the nature of commutation in all these senses: on the commutative relationships between the three thousand ducats, the friendship of Antonio and Bassanio, the pound of flesh, the life of Antonio, the livelihood of Shylock, the wedding ring of Portia, and the body of Portia in marriage; between the ducats and the daughter, between inanimate metal, dead meat, live flesh, and the living spirit. The play is most deeply about how sacrifice is the meaning of meaning. What it implies for our own time is that the death of sacrifice is the death of meaning; that the crisis in modern philosophy over the meaning of the word *reference*—and this is the heart of it—has its roots in the denial of shame and thus the denial of commutativeness; and that for reference and meaning to come back to life, some deep sacrifice is required. Perhaps that sacrifice has been made already in this century, and it is for us to recognize it as such.

The invention of ritual sacrifice, or rather perhaps its elaboration and adaptation from the division of the spoils of the hunt and the disposal of the bodies of the dead, may have begun a process of increasing suppression of the protohuman eugenics I have described. The commutation process gradually took the teeth out of social selection. Instead of the normal expulsion or killing of the polluted, there was occasional human sacrifice; instead of actual human sacrifice, scapegoat animals were killed. More and more egalitarian religious ideas arose, as in the antielitist cults of Krishna and of the Buddha in the Hindu tradition, the Greco-Roman myths of the gods in disguise as beggars, the later cults of Mithras and of popular Egyptian deities, the social criticism of the Hebrew prophets, and the Christian warning that the last shall be first and the first last. A larger and larger proportion of the population was permitted to have offspring. Tribalism came to be despised. Arranged marriage ceased to be the norm. Aristocratic ideas of the inheritance of good blood went into decline. Meanwhile a celibate priesthood came into being in many traditions, clearly and unambiguously signaling that reproductive success was no longer the reward for ritual excellence.

We rightly condemn eugenics and applaud the increasing humaneness—the humanity—of the emerging civilized morality. The word *human* itself means the rejection of the terrible process by which we became human. And if commutation in this sense also means meaning, then meaning is in another way the same thing as sacrifice.

But if we think we can safely suppress the memory of how we became human, and of the price of our new freedom, we are quite wrong. To reject such practices should not mean to repress them from our memory; and if we forget them, the basis of our shame and also the basis of our beauty as the paragon of animals, we may, in some time of terrible stress, find ourselves repeating them. And we are indeed at this time trying to repress them. The symptoms of that repression are manifold: our contemporary hatred of technology (while we use it only the more avidly); our attempt to make sexual intercourse shameless by detaching it psychologically from reproduction, family, deep and emotional commitments, the possibility of disease, and any implication of psychobiological differentiation between the sexes; our bad conscience about racism, animal "rights," and abortion; our inability to face the meaning of the Nazi Holocaust; and the element of rabid superstition in our fear that we are destroying Mother Nature. And we have few rituals left to enable us to accept and take on the burden of our inescapable impurity.

In giving up *tribal* eugenics we have irrevocably declared our commitment to technology. As civilization matured, as we have seen, it kept the routine *individual* eugenics implicit in the choice of reproductive partner; in one sense we could say that the move toward civilization is a move toward an increasing democratization of reproductive choice. Instead of the tribal collectivity deciding who should not have children, we all did, individually, by discriminating against all other potential reproductive partners than the ones we chose. The selective process was thus rendered weaker, more subtle, less consistent, and much more variable.

In contemporary society, where casual sexual promiscuity, medical intervention, and birth control tend to frustrate the process of genetic selection through reproductive success, we are in the process of giving up even the individual option for selecting and passing on valued information by genetic means. Still, over the last few thousand years we have been developing other means of passing on such information: oral poetry, writing, the arts, organized social institutions, and now computers and other advanced electronic technology. These systems have become the DNA of a new, inconceivably swifter and more complex form of life, a new twist in the evolutionary spiral.

Furthermore, we will soon be in a position to correct by means of gene therapy the diseases, distortions, and deficits that would once have condemned a cave dweller to exposure, exile, or ritual sacrifice. Thus technology, especially biotechnology, is the opposite and alternative to eugenics, which is the ancient aristocratic theory of species improvement. Technology is a further development of the evolutionary process of meaning. In this light the deconstruction of the European Jews by the Nazis appears as a hideous throwback, a deliberate reversal of all that humanity has gained in the last three million years. By means of technology, which is our *substitute* for tribal genetic activism, the worst members of the species scapegoated and fed to a hideously sanitized and deritualized holocaust a large moiety of the best. And the Jews' de facto forgiveness of the rest of the human race, if that is how we are to take it, would be the beginning of the redemption of humankind and the rebirth of beauty.

I do not present the foregoing discussion of the complex relations of sacrifice, evolution, and meaning as an assertion of a clear moral position—because, as such, whatever moral outcome we chose would involve a tragic revulsion against other moral principles we hold to be of unchallengeable validity. For instance, if we choose the ancient tribal values of the human species, we must also choose collective eugenics, racism, and blood sacrifice—or contrive somehow to detach the parts of this package, thus denaturing them of their moral weight. If we choose reproductive freedom, we must also choose advanced informational and biological technology, and find some way of dealing with a human neuropsychological makeup that needs families and primary caregivers. The only proper way to make such an argument is perhaps in a tragic play; but tragic drama requires for its audience a society that has some intellectual grasp of the necessary irreconcilability of our moral and logical conflicts. This book is intended as a step toward such an understanding; and if it could be a preface to a true tragic drama, it would have fulfilled the true function of literary criticism, which is to enable beauty to be born out of its own despairing shame.

Two further points need to be made about the biology of beauty before we can sum up this part of the argument. The first concerns beauty as a pleasure, the second beauty as analogous to, and a further development of, perception.

The experience of beauty is among other things a pleasure. It is now known that such pleasure is mediated by a highly complex brain chemistry involving at least two groups of neuropeptides, the endorphins and the enkephalins. These complex molecules are produced as the result of certain activities and experiences in the body or brain, bind to receptor sites in the neuron, and change its activity; either helping to facilitate the transfer of electrochemical information across the synapses, or as the sign to call a halt to a completed exchange of stimuli throughout a given system of neural pathways—a completion that we perhaps feel as the satisfaction of coming to a conclusion, as Frank Kermode's "sense of an ending." It is the off-switch we have that the Turing machine doesn't.

The neuropeptides are also known to be implicated in laying down the initial tracks that the dendrites will follow, as they connect the neurons up with each other in the fetal and infant brain. They can also help alter the shape of the synaptic cleft so as to make it permanently more transmissive—in other words, they help lay down memories—and they catalyze the molecular component of memory (part of memory is recorded, much as DNA records biological memory, in complex, long-chain molecules). The neuropeptides also seem to have a role in activating and toning up the immune system, and thus pleasure is not only a result of health but a cause. They also help to control the hormone system of the body, whereby we mature and attain sexual readiness; and are even subtly implicated in the brain's perception of the passing of time.

Another way of putting all this is to say that pleasure, and in particular the pleasure of beauty, is a reward that the brain is designed to give itself for the accomplishment of certain creative tasks. Addictive drugs, such as heroin and cocaine, mimic the pleasure peptides in their molecular structure, and thus interfere with the brain's own motivational system: literally stealing the soul by subverting the purpose of pleasure. The pleasure of eating clearly rewards the effort and concentration of foraging; the pleasure of sex rewards the metabolically expensive process of finding a mate and reproducing the species. What does the pleasure of beauty reward, so very highly developed in human beings, so strongly selected for by human evolution, so subtle and fugitive, so easily suppressed when we deny the shame of our existence, and yet so irresistible when it has us in its power?

Before we can begin to answer this question we need one more piece of the biological puzzle. Let us play with an idea of Kant's and see where we get if we treat the experience of beauty as something analogous to, but higher than, feeling a sensation or perceiving an object. Imagine dropping a rock on the floor. The rock *reacts,* perhaps, by bouncing and by making a noise, but we would not imagine that the rock feels anything.

Now imagine that we drop a worm on the floor; the impact might cause it to squirm, as well as merely bounce and produce a sound of impact. The worm, we would say, *feels a sensation;* but from the worm's point of view it is not a sensation of anything in particular; the worm does not construct, with its primitive nerve ganglia, anything like an external world filled with objects like floors and experimenters.

Now imagine that we drop a guinea pig. Clearly it would react as the rock does, and also feel sensations as the worm does. But we would say in addition that it *perceives* the floor, the large dangerous animal that has just released it, and the dark place under the table where it may be safe. Perception is as much beyond sensation as sensation is beyond mere physical reaction. Perception constructs a precise, individuated world of solid objects out there, endowed with color, shape, smell, and acoustic and tactile properties. It is generous to the outside world, giving it properties it did not necessarily possess until some advanced vertebrate was able, through its marvelously parsimonious cortical world-construction system, to provide them. Perception is both more global, more holistic, than sensation—because it takes into account an entire outside world—and more exact, more particular, for it recognizes individual objects and parts of objects.

Now if we were a dancer and the creature that we dropped were a human being, a yet more astonishing capacity comes into play. One could write a novel about how the dance partners experience this drop, this gesture. Whole detailed worlds of implication, of past and future, of interpretive frames come into being; and the table, the dancing floor, do not lose any of the guinea pig's reality, but instead take on richnesses, subtleties, significant details, held as they are within a context vaster and more clearly understood.

What is this awareness that is to perception what perception is to sensation, and sensation to reaction? The answer is the beauty experience. The beauty experience is as much more constructive, as much more generous to the outside world, as much more holistic and as much more exact and particularizing than ordinary perception, as ordinary perception is than mere sensation. Beauty-perception is not a vague and touchy-feely thing relative to ordinary perception; quite the reverse. This is why, given an infinite number of theories that will logically explain the facts, scientists will sensibly always choose the most beautiful theory. For good reason: because this is the way the world works.

Nor is the dancer, because he or she is a self-aware human being, any the less a perceiving animal like the guinea pig, or a sensing organism like the worm, or a piece of matter subject to, and a source of, the physical effects of electromagnetism and gravitation, like the rock. In fact part of the richness of his or her experience lies in the dissonances between those levels—the determinism of the world of kinetic energy as against the freedom of the world of dancerly expressiveness, the wormlike solipsism of the bruised cells of the foot as against the mammal awareness of the room, its colors and light and movement. And herein lies the accepted shame of the dancer's art, the athletic body pushed to its limits, the bead of sweat, the straining tendon; the high excitement of mastery almost compromised by the autonomous tremor of a muscle, the unearthly grace given pathos by the soft bulge of breast or manly sex.

Beauty in this view is the highest integrative level of understanding and the most comprehensive capacity for effective action. It enables us to go with, rather than against, the deepest tendency or theme of the universe: to be able to model what will happen and adapt to or change it. It integrates or focuses the different levels of reality, while recognizing their conflicts, as in the martial arts, where spiritual, mental, emotional and physical energies are concentrated together into the perfect strike or block. Such benefits might well be worth the enormous metabolic expense of the brain, that organ that spends a third of the body's oxygen and sugar, and for which the body will willingly sacrifice itself.

What, then, to conclude, is the pleasure of beauty a reward for? First, for the exercise of the peculiar spiritual skills demanded by the human ritual; second, for the encounter with, acceptance, and passing-through of the shame of mortal self-awareness; third, for a special integrative sensibility that is partly anticipated in the instinctive preferences of animals, a sensitivity to the general tendency or theme of the universe, its self-organizing process; and fourth, for the exercise of the human capacity to continue and deepen that process into new realms of being.

Four

The Neurocharms

IF THE theory of the biocultural evolution of the sense of beauty through traditional ritual is correct, we might expect to see a specific set of capabilities, based on new or revised neural structures in the hominid brain, that would be culturally universal and fundamental to the human arts. If an animal species, exploiting an available ecological niche, develops a particular habit of life, then it evolves special neurobiological capabilities to support it; the hawk, for instance, requires a sophisticated spatial ability, an instinctive kinetic sense for evaluating winds and thermal air currents, a powerful fine-detail and fine-movement long-distance visual system, and so on. Parts of the hawk brain have expanded relative to those of its ancestors in order to accommodate the extra hardware required. The very complex human habit of life, based primarily, as I argue, upon the sense of beauty, would require equivalent capabilities, each with brain structures of its own. This chapter is an attempt to list and classify them.

What should we call these special human abilities? They would be much more powerful and more sharply focused than the general processing of the basic mammalian brain. Perhaps we could call them hereditary knowledges, or lores, or skills, or powers, though each of these terms is misleadingly limited in one way or another. Or perhaps we should call them genres, because they have distinct forms and even rules and need a cultural feedback loop of imitation and instruction to bring out their full power. If we were to imagine certain abilities of this kind that we might have, but don't, their extraordinary dexterity might be better appreciated. We can learn, paradoxically, to recognize how wonderful are our eyes, by imagining what it would be like to have magnifying or telescopic lenses—which we might have, but don't; but we do have color perception, our natural spectrograph; and a powerful instinctive capacity for the interpretation of complex projective geometry; and a wonderful movement sensor.

But the natural capacities of beauty—and their absence in many parts of the field of possible experience and action—are even more remarkable. For instance, if our species had evolved in a highly mechanized biocultural milieu, it could easily have developed a skill for instant, easy, and unconscious calculation of mathematical problems. Just by an act of intention as simple as raising one's arm, one could bring to one's mind the value of pi, or of the square root of two, to any desired decimal place; or rattle off the first three hundred prime numbers. We regularly, as in the calculation of the grammar of our language as we speak, or in the evaluation of speeds and vectors in a busy intersection, perform calculations at least as complex and requiring at least as much neural processing. We very nearly did develop this capacity; some idiot savants seem to have the power of instant calculation, though it looks as if other brain capacities may have had to be sacrificed in order for them to do so.

Or imagine that we could as naturally recognize or create an eight-second poetic line as we do the normal and universal three-second one. Or that we could as instinctually catch the "tune" of a piece of serial music when we have not heard it before, as we can pick up a melody based upon the universal human musical scale. Or that there is the same kind of unambiguous natural mimetic and representational referent for musical keys and phrases, preexisting musical conventions, that we find in visual outline pictures, so that programmatic or narrative music would be as easily interpreted across cultures as pictorial representations are. Or that the meaning of such works as Spenser's *The Faerie Queene* or Joyce's *Finnegans Wake,* aspects of which appeal to hypothetical but not actual human linguistic abilities, should be as transpicuous to the general understanding as those of Homer, Shakespeare, and Tolstoy, which are at least as complex but which are tuned to real human brain capacities.

Of course we do now have technical prostheses not given in the primary gene-culture system, by which we can supplement the limitations of the human brain: computers to do calculations, techniques of musical and literary analysis, concordances, "skeleton keys," and so on. We also seem to be able to make one mental skill partly substitute for another. Professional musicians, who by musicological training have mapped their musical skills onto linguistic abilities, have been shown to use their linguistic left brain at least as much as the right brain in listening to music, whereas laypersons tend to use the right brain exclusively for this purpose. In mathematics algebra can serve when multidimensional topology goes beyond the human spatial instincts, and contrariwise geometry— and now its extension in mathematical computer graphics—can bring a dry numerical sequence or algebraic formula to life in such a way that new ideas open up for the mathematician. Koen de Pryck, in an as yet unpublished doctoral dissertation, has shown that dysphasic children unable to perceive the meaning of linguistic metaphors can come to understand them by drawing them on a piece of paper. One implication of this line of thought is that these powers do not cover the entire range of possible human cognition, perception, and action. They leave gaps, which can be covered partly by makeshift combinations of the canonical abilities and partly by technological crutches and aids.

But the very fact that we must go to such lengths in the absence of one of these natural powers shows how powerful, how magical, they are. We do not normally notice them precisely because they are so easy to use; but in order to understand the nature of beauty we are going to have to recognize and appreciate them for what they are. For they are all essentially aesthetic, in the best sense of that word; their cognitive and practical uses are secondary. The self-rewarding feedback system, and the acceleration of insight and spiritual force that we feel in the full current of one of the natural-classical artistic genres, either as creator or audience, only happens there, and not in the gaps between them. Modernist art set itself to see with new eyes; but the new prosthetic eyes are not as good as the old ones, unless—and this anticipates one of the conclusions of this book—we can find a way to plug the new eyes into the old. The old eyes are our natural magic. Perhaps, then, the magical term *spells* would be a more accurate word for them—neurospells, biospells—or *runes* as in the old Norse magic. But these terms are a little too linguistic in flavor. We shall settle, then, for the word *charms,* in the combination *neurocharms.* This word implies not only a linguistic element, but also a musical one (as in its cognate *carmen,* song) and a visual one (as in a magic charm one might wear on one's wrist or breast or temple). Likewise, the word can refer to an ability, to an experience, and to the feeling of pleasure that rewards us for either. For the Greeks they were the muses and the graces, and the experience of them is most like a mild divine possession.

The development of these neurocharms in the course of mammalian, primate, and human evolution required a massive enlargement and modification of parts of the brain. Much of the huge human neocortex, whose folds swelled out through the generations to envelop the older parts of the brain, is now known to be given over to one or another of them. The limbic system, that lobed inner hem of the cortex, anatomically specialized into a series of bulbs, bridges, and prongs, was gradually transformed from what was primarily a smell-interpretation system into the center of affect and motivation, the gatekeeper or editor of memory, the monitor of the body's internal states, and the dispenser of pleasurable reward. And an enormous web of neural connections was laid down between the limbic system (especially its core and switchboard the hypothalamus), and the frontal association cortex in the forebrain, where reside the functions of conscious thought, mental reflection, creative insight, and personal decision. This connection, between emotion and reason, so to speak, is among the closest in the brain; from an anatomic point of view they are virtually two parts of the same organ. As Walle J. H. Nauta and Michael Feirtag put it in their textbook *Fundamental Neuroanatomy:*

The orbital part of the frontal cortex—alone in the neocortex—projects to the hypothalamus. Thus the limbic system founders as a circumscribed part of the brain, quite distinct from the neocortex. After all, the modern criterion for membership in the limbic system is a synaptic proximity to the hypothalamus, and the frontal cortex has that. In fact it has uninterrupted access to the visceral, endocrine, and affective mechanisms of the hypothalamic continuum. No other part of the neocortex has access so direct. What, then, is the frontal cortex? In the first place, the frontal cortex has long been notable for its lack of primary sensory fields. It is entirely association cortex. Indeed, as we have noted, the tracing of large-scale projections in the white matter underlying the cerebral cortex suggests that the frontal cortex is a neocortical end of the line: it is a destination for sequential projections that begin in the primary sensory fields. Second, the frontal cortex is a destination for signals with antecedents in the primary olfactory cortex [the limbic affective-motivational system]. (New York: Freeman, 1986, p. 130)

It is also known that the frontal association cortex is essential in transforming knowledge into action; and so if we put together the functions of receiving the final products of sensory perception from the rest of the cortex, complex and self-reflective reassociation of these products, emotional and pleasurable response to the results, "gut feelings" or somatic hunches from the evolutionary history of the species, motivation, decision-making, and creative action, we have what is close to a recipe for the artistic process. (The work of Robin Fox and Lionel Tiger on the brain and culture is especially illuminating in this connection.)

The neurocharms divide themselves first of all into two large groups, the left-brain group and the right-brain group. The right-brain group in turn divides itself into two subgroups, one developed out of auditory, or musical, information-processing, and one developed out of visual, or pictorial, information-processing.

In Homo sapiens all the neurocharms in the left-brain group

have increasingly been subsumed into and dominated by what we might call the supercharm, language. They are as follows:

1. Syntactical organization
2. Trope, symbol, metaphor, and various forms of reference
3. Collecting, selecting, classification, and hierarchical taxonomy
4. Dramatic mimesis, the power of inter- and intrapersonal reflection and modeling
5. Debate, dialectic, and eristics
6. Divination, hypothesis, and metaphysical synthesis, the scientific imagination
7. Narrative, story, and myth

The auditory right-brain group is as follows:

8. Musical meter, tempo, and rhythm
9. Musical tone, melody, and harmony
10. Musical performance, the making and playing of musical instruments

The visual right-brain group is as follows:

11. Pattern recognition, detail frequency preference, visual rhythm, and composition
12. Color; the recognition and creation of meaningful combinations of colors
13. The eye-hand mimetic capacity: picturing

In addition, there are five other neurocharms, three of which mediate between the groups listed above, as follows:

14. Dance, gymnastics, and the martial arts. (This charm mediates between the visual right-brain group and the auditory right-brain group.)
15. The ideographic, geometrical, architectonic, mapping capacity. (This charm mediates between the right-brain visual group and the left-brain linguistic group, and is the basis of writing.)

16. Poetic meter, cadence, and the art of vocal expression. (This charm mediates between the right-brain auditory group and the left-brain linguistic group.)

Another charm, which does not fit into any of the main groups, is a sort of marvelous by-product of the rewiring of the olfactory (smell) and taste centers of the mammal brain as an emotional and motivational system:

17. Cuisine and its derivative arts, the appreciation and making of wines, perfumes, cheeses, etc.

A final charm is based upon the mammalian and primate grooming rituals:

18. The art of massage, therapeutic manipulation, physical nurturing, and sexual intercourse

In addition, we possess a strange and inbuilt capacity to recognize uses of fundamental paradox or self-inclusion, and to transcend them without abolishing them: laughter. Laughter is the raw form of the beauty experience itself: it is to beauty as sexual arousal is to love. There are other charms besides, but I believe that we share them in an unchanged or perhaps diminished state with other mammals, and they have not been through the ritual acceleration into the realm of human beauty.

Before we go on to look at some of these genres in detail, let us point out certain features that stand out when we see them all together. One is that each involves a full range of sensory, cognitive, affective, communicative, and motor capacities. Even the more abstract linguistic charms are strongly connected with the senses and motor system through metaphor and the drive to experiment.

Another general feature is that although the language group is obviously the single largest set of neurocharms, it is not by any means the only paradigm of knowledge and communication. In this classification, which is no doubt incomplete in places and confused in others, there are seven charms associated with each cerebral hemisphere, left and right (on the right, three visual, three auditory, and one crossover); there are two crossover charms between left and right, and two more charms, associated with other aspects of the evolved brain. Thus the linguistic charms are in the minority, and the heavily linguistic model of postmodern critical theory and aesthetics is evidently a distortion, based perhaps on a desire to deny the shame of bodily existence and the somatic incarnation of our identity.

At the same time, however, we must reject yet another modernist attempt at oversimplification: that thought is limiting, dry, rational, linear, and alienating, while emotion is open-ended, rich, sensual, nonlinear, and holistic. The fact that the higher associative centers are most deeply connected to the emotional and somatic limbic system, that they are the final destination of all sensory information, and that they represent the summation of the whole brain's work should belie any such strategy to separate self-consciousness, conscience, and judgment from the shameful things which are to be judged.

Another feature that stands out when we consider the neurocharms all together is that there is a sort of parallelism between the musical group and the visual group; musical rhythm corresponds to visual texture (or detail frequency), and musical tonality corresponds to color. Likewise, and rather interestingly, the capacity for musical performance seems to match the capacity for visual representation and picture-making. I believe that these correspondences reflect similar evolutionary histories in the neural specialization of the visual and auditory cortexes. The same kind of distinctions of function may even hold for the linguistic left-brain; it is an area for research.

A final feature is that all of these charms involve a full cooperation between a biogenetic endowment and a cultural tradition that can activate and shape it. We all have neural organs adaptively designed for the purpose of language, but also require the environment of a specific natural language to awaken them. The same applies to the skills of melody and harmony, of poetic meter and visual representation, of theatrical performance and cookery.

This biocultural feedback loop can generate extraordinarily various forms once it is established; but if the basic training in the charms is neglected, they will never show what they can do. An education that neglected them in the name of diversity or flexibility would leave the student bereft of magic and incapable of true cultural invention.

Five

The Language Group

SYNTAX. The human capacity to generate syntax is a nice example of how we can possess an apparently magical power and not notice it until someone, like Noam Chomsky, points it out. Syntax shows clearly the principles that govern all the neurocharms. It has a clear neurobiological substrate that is culturally universal, with its own identifiable brain structure, known as Broca's area, on the left front part of the brain, part of the association cortex. It has rules within each culture that must be learned. It is generative, that is, a small number of elements and rules can produce an infinite and flexible variety of expressions. It is hierarchical in structure, but the hierarchy is flexible and adapted to its function. And it divides up the fields of space and time in a way which is beautiful in itself and which also provides privileged and distinct locations for the establishment, storage, transformation, and retrieval of meaning. This last is another way of putting the fact that the basic act of human value-creation is a self-reflexive elaboration of a condition of physical being.

The etymological roots of the word *grammar* show that the ancients were not ignorant of the magical and artistic powers of grammar: the Greek *grammatike* meant the art of letters, and the Middle English *gramarye* (from which we get glamour), meant magic or necromancy.

Trope. Of all the fundamental intellectual problems that have dogged modernity, the issue of reference may be the most intractable. The difficulty is based on the fallacy that words and things are two different and incommensurate orders of being, and that the thing in itself is either inaccessible to us (because we cannot but think in language) or, as in the poststructuralist consensus, absent altogether. This is a fallacy not only because it assumes the total dominance of verbal left-brain language in cognition but also because it unconsciously assumes that a thing is, or ought to be, an independent substance in itself, whereas a word is just an airy tag that we stick on it. If things in this sense do not exist, then all there is, is the airy tags, the play of *écriture,* of deferral and difference, of archetraces, in their hermeneutic and politically determined circle. If things in this sense do exist, like the female body in French feminist theory, they must be inchoate, unformed, indescribable by tropes, that to which no reference can be made, since reference hierarchizes and kills.

This position—or rather, this complementary pair of positions—neglects another possibility, which is that tropes do often, though not always, correctly refer, and that reference is a concrete and concretizing feature of the natural world. It assumes that information (form) and being (matter) are distinct categories, when in fact being is made of information, matter is made of form.

As we know, matter is simply energy bound up in a field structure; the field structure is the language that makes energy behave as matter. This binding into matter does not make energy less real, but more real—exactly C^2 times more real, according to the formula $E = MC^2$, where C is the speed of light. The code of the DNA molecule, which is detachable from any particular material embodiment of it—in theory one could record the code of a living organism in a computer and then rebuild it with chemicals from the shelf—is the language that makes matter behave as life. But life, troped matter as it is, is not the less real than untroped matter for its having been troped, but more real. Human language makes life behave as mind, as DNA makes matter behave as life, and field structure makes energy behave as matter; and so language is a partially constitutive element of the being of the named world.

It is important that it is only partly constitutive: like the form of DNA or even of a space-time field, language is detachable from its

THE LANGUAGE GROUP / 71

various substrates, or referents, and does not necessarily enact what it stipulates; all the sociolinguistic consensus in the world will not make us fall up if we jump out of a ten-story window. We did not invent the forms of space-time or of DNA, though we can, if we understand them, modify them within limits. We could devise a strand of DNA in a computer that would specify a nonexistent and nonviable animal (one with both more and less than three legs, perhaps, or one with an inside but no outside). We can likewise invent metaphysical or metacritical theories that do not refer to any actual entity or work of art. Some of these might stipulate a viable reality, as one day we will perhaps devise viable animals in a computer. But other theories, or chimeras, might not fit the existing ecology. The physical world already possesses a powerful consensus of its own, to which we must adapt and out of which we grow. Our performative statements work only when they do not contradict that consensus and when, through their beauty, they can attract a consensus of their own among human beings and other entities in the world.

The troping charm, the power to make similes, metaphors, metonyms, symbols, and so on, is the way in which we permit the physical world to take on yet another shell of reality and increase its concreteness by another jump. By poetic symbolization the world takes on new meanings and coherence; by mathematical symbolization (algebra) the world takes on, through the technology that algebra makes possible, new activities and operations. A major new trope is like a major new natural species that has just evolved; the ecosystem adjusts to make room for it, or perhaps, if it is inefficient, suppresses it. As we have already noted, there is in the heart of the troping process an element of sacrificial commutation, of sacrificial shame and epiphany.

There is a logic in the use of tropes that we glimpse sometimes in its absence, in the ugliness of a mixed metaphor. That logic was the subject of a highly developed theory in the late Middle Ages and the Renaissance that embraced parts of the disciplines of rhetoric, astronomy, medicine, alchemy, theology, and philosophy; today the science of it is almost lost. We can, perhaps, see the beginnings of a revival of that science in some of the results of contemporary psycholinguistics.

For instance, R. H. J. Williams has discovered a humanly universal directionality in which metaphors drawn from one sense are usually applied to describe another. Touch metaphors often describe a taste, a color, or a sound (a sharp tang of lime, a soft blue, a rasping noise). Taste metaphors usually only describe smells (a sweet perfume, sour odors), and smell metaphors do not seem to be often used for other senses; in fact we do not have much in the way of a specific smell vocabulary at all, reflecting the paucity of direct neural connections between the olfactory and linguistic regions of the brain. Dimensional metaphors can describe colors or sounds (a deep red, high C), and color and sound metaphors can describe each other (bright orchestration, the blues, loud colors). From these observations we can extrapolate a series of senses: touch, taste, smell, dimension, and color or sound (color and sound seem to occupy the same position in the sequence). Metaphorization operates commonly only in this sequence—that is, we do not normally describe a touch or a taste in terms of a color or sound (a red taste, a loud touch, a broad savor). Of course poetry can often strikingly reverse the default sequence of the brain, but to know the difference would be a valuable part of the craft of trope. The normal sequence of metaphorical transfer also happens to recapitulate the sequence of phylogenetic development of the senses in animals and human beings; to quote from Heinrich Zollinger, to whom I owe much of this discussion: "The hindbrain of early vertebrates processes touch, taste, and balance. The midbrain of higher vertebrates is specialized in processing olfactory and visual stimuli. The acoustic sense probably developed parallel to the visual sense. This leads to a sequence of sense development from touch to taste, smell, and finally, to hearing and sight" (Heinrich Zollinger, "Biological Aspects of Color Naming," in *Beauty and the Brain: Biological Aspects of Aesthetics,* ed. Ingo Rentschler, Barbara Herzberger, and David Epstein [Basel, Boston, Berlin: Birkhauser Verlag, 1988], p. 162).

The new evolutionary picture of the universe that is emerging from the sciences may help us to construct the equivalent of a Great Chain of Being for our own times, and recover the unity of cosmos and psyche that is the birthright of cultures all over the world. We need a Thomas Aquinas to map it out, a Dante to make it poetically real. But such a shaman will have to encounter the full fury of those who, in fear of the shame of our incarnate nature, have invested their lives in the meaninglessness and illegitimacy of meaning and reference.

Taxonomy. The Indo-European root *leg-,* which originally referred to the process of picking out seeds and which perhaps goes all the way back to the seed-, firewood-, root-, fruit-, and nut-gathering activity of a hunter-gatherer species, has given us many words that refer to the skills of careful choice and arrangement out of a range of possibilities. The way the word has extended itself metaphorically is very revealing: collect, select, sortilege, sacrilege, lexicon, dialogue, dyslexia, legal, delegate, logic, logos, syllogism, logarithm. We see it at its best in the great classification systems of Linnaeus and of the nineteenth-century German philologists; it is an essential element in any large-scale work of art, in which the parts must be harmoniously related to the whole. Clearly related to the syntactical-grammatical charm, this power enables us to sort things out into groups and hierarchies, so that we can concentrate on one or contemplate the whole. It is also very closely connected to the architectonic-diagrammatic charm, which we will look at later.

Because classification systems differ across the world, scholars in the West, which was the first major culture area to attempt a deep and genuine understanding of other cultures, were initially inclined to exclaim about the radical incommensurability of different cultural "worlds." Together with the salutary scientific humility of this stance, there was for the great ethnographers also the satisfaction of amazing and bewildering the home population with their knowledge of arcane secrets from afar, which by implication rendered all its own customs arbitrary and ridiculously overearnest. What is now becoming clear, however, is how astonishingly universal those classification systems are under the surface. But this universality, and the inherent contradiction in the scholars' claims of hermeneutic incommensurability (how would one know how different those cultural worlds were unless one had bridged them?) was not noticed by the general population, partly because it was already looking for ways to evade the shame of its own traditions.

Modernist theoreticians attempted to separate language and its attendant classification systems from its shameful neurobiological basis, so that the moral and aesthetic judgmental categories they contained would be culturally relative and so defused of normative force. They thus seized on what came to be known as the Sapir-Whorf hypothesis, which was an interesting theory, of limited validity, to the effect that the differences between languages reflected fundamental variations in cultural worldview. Further anthropological-linguistic research (for instance, by the anthropologist Donald Brown), has shown that anything that can be said or thought in one language can be said or thought in another, though some paraphrase may be necessary. We all basically have the same worldview, as far as linguistic differences are concerned.

But the news of this correction has not yet seeped through to most contemporary pundits of aesthetic theory, and the old clichés of the thirty-four Eskimo words for snow and the lack of a past and future tense in some Plains Indians languages are still trotted out as evidence of the incommensurability of different cultural "worlds" (and thus of the arbitrariness of value judgments). We can forgive someone like Wittgenstein for the idea of different language games, given the state of anthropological and neuropsychological research in his times; it is harder, however, to forgive contemporary cultural relativists who should by now know better.

Mimesis. One of our most remarkable capacities is our ability to adopt the point of view of other persons, even to the extent of introjecting their personalities and being able to hear their voices in our heads. The modeled versions of others that we carry within us have their own fictional inventiveness and can in turn model what they think we are thinking, and the model of us that they create in turn carries a little model of them. Even when we are alone we can generate a multitude of selves: the self that desires something, the superego-self that condemns the desire, the psychotherapist-self that undermines the superego-self, the cultural critic-self that questions the wisdom of the psychotherapist-self, and so on.

The mathematical psychologist Vladimir Lefebvre has shown that these halls of reflecting psychic mirrors work by a kind of Boolean logic, each layer of criticism adding a smaller increment of change to our cumulative attitude, an attitude that approaches, when averaged out, a sort of default-judgment toward things in general that is about 61.8 percent positive and 38.2 percent negative. This ratio happens, very interestingly, to be that of the golden section, which has the unique property that the ratio of the larger of the two terms to their sum is equal to that of the smaller of the two terms to the larger: A:(A+B) :: B:A. The golden section is, as we shall see, a theme in many of the other neurocharms by which we create and perceive the beautiful.

In other words, the capacity to arrive at moral and aesthetic judgments is based upon our capacity to model, by an innate mimetic or dramatic imagination, other persons and other versions of one's own person and set them in judgment upon our behavior. Here again we are in the territory of shame, of that self-consciousness which we would escape but which makes us human. Certain lesions of the associative frontal cortex can damage this reflective aesthetic and moral conscience, so that the individual can no longer generate an internal feedback of criticism. Drug-addiction, which interferes with the brain's self-reward system, can do the same thing; and ideological commitment, which requires the comfortable silencing of certain kinds of shame and self-doubt, can do so as well.

It is evident that this mimetic-evaluative process is at the core of ritual drama and is also the basis of that tragic and comic theatrical beauty that Aristotle celebrates in his *Poetics*. Aristotle might be a good guide in an initial attempt to determine the necessary grammatical rules of this neurocharm and thus the best ways to educate ourselves in it: his stipulations about hubris, hamartia, anagnorisis, catharsis, and the beginning-middle-end structure of the tragic genre, for instance, may have some likelihood of being culturally universal and neurogenetically hardwired. It need hardly be pointed out that all these elements, and theatrical mimesis itself, have come under assault by modernist and postmodernist theatrical aesthetics.

Aristotle's weakness is not, I believe, any of those with which his recent critics have charged him. It is that like many Greek philosophers, he did not like surds, irrational numbers, infinite regresses, vicious circles, double binds, and unbounded series, and he was thus unwilling to pursue the dizzying feedback of theatrical and moral reflexivity beyond the realm of a limited and targeted growth process. The Greek *tragedians,* however, recognized those surds and regresses and accepted them intuitively as part of our shame and as implicit in the very dynamic of creative evolution, which goes beyond growth to the emergence of new species of reality. Euripides' Pentheus fights those reflective and fractal dragons unsuccessfully in *The Bacchae,* and Sophocles shows us how Oedipus achieves wisdom through his encounter with them, in his short-circuited kinship relationships and in the bewilderingly reflexive predicting-contest he loses to the oracles of Apollo.

Debate. Closely related to the power of dramatic mimesis, but involving a special charm of its own, is the dialectical, or eristic, muse. One of the characteristics of a neurocharm is that once it is in operation it performs almost automatically, magically, like walking or breathing. If we have the right training in logic and argument, our compulsion to continue a debate is almost druglike, and our capacity to do so seems inexhaustible. There is always another turn of the dialectical spiral that will show us to be right, and this twisting of thought fascinates us. Here those who are not greatly gifted in the charm, or have missed the training, fail to understand the eristic motivation and attribute it to macho or to defensive self-righteousness. It is not the being right that is important but the sheer possibilities of unexplored argument, the labyrinth of new ideas that is opened up. This neurocharm is one of the few that has survived, relatively undamaged, the modernist and postmodernist assaults. But deconstruction may be the end of the line, for though its motive is often splendidly eristic, its final argument is to discredit the logic in which argument can take place and the clarity of language and sequence that constitutes the game's field of play.

Divination-hypothesis. If the taxonomic charm is the drive to know what is the structure of a mass of details, the divinatory-hypothetical charm is the desire to know *why*. We must always make sense of the world and find in it an explanation that is simpler and more elegant than simply the ensemble of all of its details. Whether that explanation is the ancestors, or the gods, or God, or the laws of motion, or the geometry of space-time, or the conspiracy of a property-owning class, or dialectical reason working itself out in history, or repressed libido, or the theory of evolution by natural selection, we seek elegant hypotheses that can act as a sharp fulcrum and give us leverage to move the world.

This neurocharm has a peculiar history, if my analysis of it is correct. That is, I believe that the same brain structures and specialized functions are involved in reading horoscopes, palms, entrails, bird omens, tea leaves, the contents of divinatory baskets, and the I Ching as are involved in forming a scientific or philosophical hypothesis to explain a large body of puzzling observation and experiment. In just the same fashion the thinker accumulates an uncomfortably large body of facts, most of which are not strictly relevant; and then, in a flash of insight, or even in a dream, the meaning becomes clear and everything falls into place. Perhaps the true function of the huge mass of disparate information that surrounds any flash of divinatory insight—whether that insight is a person's future, or a medical diagnosis, or a mathematical explanation of natural phenomena—is to stimulate the brain until some threshold of connectivity is reached, to be followed by the rapid selection of the most beautiful idea and the collapse of all the facts into a new order. The experience resembles that of laughter. It is in a sense a kind of amazing luck that when this powerful ability is paired with careful experiment and the recording of the results, and assisted by the taxonomic, dialectical, ideographic, and narrative charms, it becomes a reliable means to ascertain the nature of the physical universe.

One of the problems for the modernity implicit in the workings and history of this charm is that it often implies superordinate norms and points of view and moral ideals in whose imagined eyes we stand shamed and all too human. Even if that superordinate explanation is a structure as abstract as space-time, we are shamed by our very consciousness, by our messy physicality, and by our timebound nature in a universe whose norm is clean geometry, impersonality, and a kind of eternity in which time is equivalent to space. Three strategies to avoid metaphysical shame have developed in our epoch. The first was the fascist social morality, in which the shaming and subordinate aspects of nature and of human nature were projected upon the Other and rabidly persecuted. The second, which was in many ways similar to the first but with different targets, was the theory of leftist terror exemplified in the idea of revolutionary honor, the works of Franz Fanon, and the remarkable film *The Battle of Algiers*. Here one *became* the theory, one utterly subordinated oneself, with a sweet abandon, to the superordinate norm, rejecting one's own personal identity as bourgeois false consciousness. Bauhaus architecture is another version of this terror.

The third, quite different, strategy was existentialism, which denied the existence of any larger and more elegant explanation, any essence, any norm or higher point of view. If we blinded our metaphysical eyes, we would not see our nakedness. But the principle "existence before essence" is still, paradoxically, an explanatory principle; and a new kind of shame was invented, the shame of the irrepressible speculative imagination, which knows that it is showing its culpable weakness by continuing to think and hypothesize, and stands shamed and naked before the disapproving gaze of the correct existentialist. Woody Allen delightfully catches this new shame in his short story "The Whores of Mensa," in which male closet intellectuals, bored with their sensual and existentially well-adjusted wives, pay for illicit sessions of metaphysical and literary discussion with the female intellectuals of the story's title. The antimetaphysical metaphysics of existentialism continues in contemporary postmodernism as, for instance, the rejection of the transcendental signifier, the delegitimation of the gaze, and the assault on logocentrism and phallocentrism. These terms are clearly loaded to the gunwales with repressed and raging shame.

Hypotheses that are untested by observation and experiment may be wrong, even if they possess a certain valid beauty of their own. Some of the forms created by the feedback system of the brain contain the power to reconnect with the rest of nature and to go on being productive into the future; but others, though they show the exquisite detail and complexity of their origin, are sterile and unproductive. Much critical and aesthetic theory, I believe, falls into this latter category. On the interpretative side this neurocharm can construct edifices as elaborate as the medical theories of prescientific societies, but which leave the patient unambiguously dead. On the creative side it can devise works of art which appeal to nonexistent capacities of the brain, whose elaborations are wasted on the dull space between one vital, sensitive neurocharm and another, and which can only be enjoyed as clumsy allegories of some kind of metaphysical, semiotic, hermeneutical, political, or deconstructionist theory.

But in the light of our analysis of the biological roots of beauty it would be an act of amputation and a denial of our humanity—a denial of our own specific animality!—to cut off the great neurocharm of hypothesis, divination, the scientific and metaphysical imagination. We can only, as human beings, be good existentialists by being good essentialists. And as Thoreau said and as William James reiterated, the world responds to our conceptions; our scientific hypotheses are sometimes right, and our metaphysical beliefs can in a limited way alter the course of events.

Story. This term is a better one than *narrative,* for the same reasons that *beauty* is better than *aesthetics.* Stories are what mommies and daddies tell their children, the way old people remember their century. A storyteller constructs a series of events that have the curious property of being retrodictable (each one seems inevitable once it has happened) but not predictable (before it happens, we have no sound basis on which to foretell it); which is why we want to know what happens next. This neurocharm comes with a large collection of archetypal myths and stories, which, as Joseph Campbell has wonderfully shown us, are fundamentally identical all over the world, because their seeds are in our genes.

Certain moments in a good story possess a quality which is logically very strange indeed and which renders them haunting and unforgettable. Consider Dorothea's choice of Ladislaw as her lover in *Middlemarch:* the logic of fiction would dictate that Dorothea would pair up with Lydgate, who is a heavyweight like her, and if after reading the first half of the book we were to try to predict the outcome, this would probably be our choice. On the other hand, when she upsets our expectations we are on reflection not disappointed but deeply excited by the depth of what has happened: strangely, we now realize that Dorothea's surprising choice was really inevitable all along, that it had to be that way; her originality, her tenderness, her St. Teresa–like sense of mastery could express itself no other way.

We get the same feeling when Edmund has his deathbed repentance in *King Lear,* and even more so when it turns out that his repentance, which would be the perfect deus ex machina to save Cordelia's life, ends up with no apparent plot function at all: in fact it makes Cordelia's death even more unexpected, arbitrary, and horrifying. Yet we recognize immediately the absolute rightness of this reversal; it was inevitable all along!

One could cite dozens of other examples: the *Odyssey* is a compendium of them, Faulkner is a master at the art, and so is Tolstoy. In music the same thing happens: Mozart will often pile two or three twists of melodic or harmonic surprise upon each other, and yet in retrospect the structure of his piece will hold firm, perfectly braced, airy, yet as strong as adamant.

The peculiar thing about such moments is that by their unpredictability before the event combined with their retrodictability after it they radically defy the requirement that truth be independent of time; and yet they are by no means arbitrary or merely expedient—it is not as if the artist were irresponsibly flinging in extraneous incident or distorting the integrity of the work by arbitrary crowd-pleasing interventions. It was Plato who most clearly established the idea that truth cannot trim its sails with the winds of time, that two and two must equal four for all eternity, not just today, or on Wednesdays, or in the past but not the future. Certainly there are kinds of coherent truth of which Plato's requirement of temporal indifference must hold. But he is perhaps wrong in implying that coherence and intelligibility—which are supreme virtues, else we could not even reason about such matters, and must come to blows—are only possible under conditions of time invariance. There are evolutionary truths as well as eternal truths; and the evolutionary truths include most of what we hold to be of value.

Edmund and Dorothea and Odysseus and Quentin Compson and Anna Karenina are coherent and intelligible—so much so that a lifetime is not enough to appreciate how much. But much of what they do has the peculiar capacity to alter the past in such a way as to make certain futures inevitable, when they were not so before. Story is part of the continuous and irreversible process of ecological change that constitutes universal evolution, but it is a part that can be miraculously retold (though it is never the same in the retelling). It is that genre by which we give time a complex tense-structure, full of might-have-beens and should-be's, conditionals, subjunctives, branches, hopes, and memories.

As with the other neurocharms, our century in its attempt to evade shame has launched an assault upon "narrativity," especially the "grand narratives" of science. But it has also found "narrative history" useful as a means of revisionism and as a rebuke to the imagined gaze of a historical point of view in whose eyes we may be shamefully inadequate. But when the historical muse, Clio, is unchained, she may work some strange and beautiful transformations. My own work with graduate students who have conducted narrative history research has shown that the stories of old-timers are full of a dignity and a shame that brings to one's face the blush of an archaic and repressed self-consciousness.

Six

The Musical Group

Musical meter. By means of this neurocharm we divide and redivide time into a complex pattern of intervals. Matching, interfering with, elaborating and harmonizing the rhythms of nature and of our own bodies, it constitutes both a reflexive comment on the rhythmic feedback of the world and a further development of it. Whereas the left-brain linguistic neurocharms often make sense of a complex spatial field of details by drawing it out into a meaningful temporal sequence, right-brain neurocharms such as this one do the opposite, and by repetition with variation are able to create meaningful spacelike structures out of temporal sequences.

We find this charm highly developed in African drum music, in rubato and other subtle techniques of variation upon and combinations of tempos in Western classical music, and in the emotional metrics of Chinese and Japanese court music. (The work of David Epstein, the musicologist, has been especially valuable here.) A piece of Indonesian gamelan music passes through a very complex pattern of rhythmic cycles that come into phase with each other only in the course of continuous repetitions, creating a kind of acoustic mandala, a description of eternity as containing time. The musicologist Jane Perry-Camp has shown in a penetrating analysis of the relationship between theme and development in the works of Mozart and others, that the golden section ratio, that familiar harmonic constant in architecture and the visual arts, is also an important unconscious attractor in the organization of musical compositions.

But musical rhythm and tempo, even as they suggest eternal perfection, carry with them an embarrassing reminder of the bodily rhythms of sex and other physical functions, and they can both evoke and stun the process of self-awareness. In the deepest sense, rhythm implies time, and time implies both consciousness and mortality. Hence our aesthetic unease about jazz and rock (words whose hypothetical derivations include slang terms for sexual intercourse). Modernist academic or "serious" music has often avoided obvious rhythmic repetition, perhaps for these reasons.

It is easy to see how this neurocharm might have evolved in the need for synchrony in tribal ritual; being on the same wave length, "in synch," is essential for the turn-taking of collective performance. This neurocharm is related to that of poetic meter and to that of dance, but it is not tuned as the former is to the needs of language, nor as the latter is to the anatomy of the moving human body; and it exists for the most part in symbiosis with the charm of musical tone, which is our next topic.

Musical tone. Musical melody and rhythm are the acoustic equivalents of forms and textures in the world of sight. If the beats of musical sound are too close together, if its rhythms are on too high a frequency for us to count them, we generalize the rhythm as a musical tone. If a visual texture is too finely woven for us to feel its rasp with the eye, what we perceive is color in the visual world. Thus with both eye and ear there are three stages of generalization: form, texture, color; and melody, rhythm, tone.

Musical tone has a long scientific history. Pythagoras' discovery of the fourfold correspondence among the numerical ratios of arithmetic, the spatial ratios of geometry, the vibratory properties of strings with different lengths, and the natural harmonic and melodic preferences of the human ear established once and for all the principle of beauty as the human way of perceiving the fundamental objective properties of reality. The cultural universality of tonality, its evident basis in human neurobiology and natural harmonics, and its substantial independence of words as a means of knowing have long been embarrassments to the arguments of the cultural determinists, who assert the linguistic and social construction of reality.

When the music of non-Western traditions first became available to Western intellectuals, it sounded sufficiently unfamiliar to support an initial judgment that music was just another social construction with no basis in human or universal nature. But our ear became accustomed to foreign melodies almost as quickly as it did to changes in our own musical fashions, and musicological analysis has shown that, as in grammar, there is a deep structure in music that is common to societies all over the world. Simple integer ratios between frequencies are universally harmonious; the overtone series is a fundamental guide to melodic success; the scale is shared by all cultures; we all crave harmonic resolution and a tonal center; wolf-notes are wolf-notes on every continent. Our cultural relativism should have been revealed as a vulgar and ignorant jumping to conclusions on the basis of a first impression.

But too much was already invested in cultural relativism for it to be abandoned so easily. It was a sovereign remedy for shame: what was wrong or ugly in one culture could be right and beautiful in another; what failed in one culture might succeed in another. The variety of culture stood as a sort of defense against our animality, our sexuality, our mortality, our failure, and our self-consciousness. We need not be ashamed of our nakedness, so to speak, if nakedness were the cultural norm in the jungle. We did not like to be told by anthropologists that, for instance, it is as shameful and sexually suggestive among the New Guinea Eipo to take off one's armband in public as it would be among ourselves to take off one's knickers; for universality gives an unwelcome legitimacy to sexual shame. Worse still, such observations showed that self-consciousness—and conscience—was not just a disease of the civilized West, which we should cure by a life of sensations rather than of thoughts, but a part of being human. Nonetheless, if aesthetics were arbitrary, then morality might be so too, and we could evade a shaming judgment on both counts.

It thus became part of the program of Western art music to prove that there was no universal and natural basis to music by creating a body of music that broke all the natural rules of the tonal neurocharm. Atonal, aleatory, and conceptual music were devised; slinkies were solemnly dropped from grand pianos. The result might have been expected; the human ear found no pleasure in it, and the Western musical culture bifurcated into "popular" and "serious" musical traditions. Jazz, the blues, rock, and other popular forms swiftly evolved into major artistic genres, melding folk art traditions with new expressive resources; and they have now begun to absorb the classical-popular-folk traditions of the Balkans, the Middle East, India, Japan, Africa, and tribal cultures all over the world. As the cultural-relativist program of "serious music" showed its bankruptcy, some "serious" composers and musicians like Philip Glass and the Chronos Quartet have begun to erase the boundary between the serious and the popular.

Meanwhile contemporary physical science has confirmed Pythagoras' vision of the universe as a vast, complex harmonic system in ways that would be beyond his wildest dreams. Superstring theory, one of our strongest attempts at a physical Theory of Everything, proposes a mathematical-geometrical model whose fundamental constituents are infinitesimal strings, the vibratory properties of which determine the nature of matter. The rules that govern chemical combinations are essentially musical; an electron in a given atomic shell is a sort of tone that can be modulated and combined according to harmonic rules. The sun is a gigantic vibrating gong, whose prodigious internal transfers of energy are accomplished by acoustic waves; and the solar system is a harmonic gravitational organism, with preferred tonal niches where the orbit of a moon or planet will be stable. There is a music of the spheres, and the ear's natural sense of beauty is also a perception of the truth.

Musical performance. The physical capacity to sing, and to construct, tune, and play musical instruments, is itself, I believe, a neurocharm of its own. Pan the god of nature is also the maker of the syrinx. The otolaryngeal system, as Harvey Wheeler has shown, evolved into a sort of model of the relations of the physical universe. Musical instruments, with their graceful, strange, and natural shapes, are the concrete metaphors through which that model finds its application and reference. Of all the neurocharms, the capacity for musical performance is perhaps the most strikingly magical; the pianist's fingers seem driven by some force of divine possession, some miraculous automatism that is clearly beyond conscious intention, at least in its details. In traditional music the whole of the tribal past with all its dead speaks through the possessed body of the performer. In classical music that tribe of dead are there also, but focused through the bright lens of a Mozart or a Bach, who come to life individually in a good performance.

This neurocharm has been little damaged by modernist and postmodernist attempts to deny our human shame, although some of the more extreme forms of "serious" music have claimed to eliminate musical virtuosity as a legitimate aesthetic goal. But it has survived, and the spontaneity of musical performance and improvisation have achieved new artistic heights in the popular genres of jazz, folk, rock and so on.

The myth of Cain, the ancestor of the first makers of musical instruments, might provide us with a clue for a hypothetical post-modern aesthetic that could achieve some temporary success, if we were mischievous enough to develop it. Musical instruments, we might suggest, are part of the patriarchal economic system, founded on Cain's violence and the intrusive technology of Tubal-Cain and his descendants. They were designed to control the body and to reinforce an arbitrary theory of time that serves the interests of the status quo and subjects us to the reifying gaze of a transcendent harmonic signifier. The valuing of musical virtuosity is a form of coercion against those who will not adapt their bodies to the implied musical metaphysic. This sort of argument, which may sound delightfully loony when applied to musical skill, is regularly used in all seriousness by critical theorists of narrative and poetic meter.

Seven

The Visual Group

Pᴀᴛᴛᴇʀɴ. The following discussion owes much to the advice and research of the psychophysicist Ingo Rentschler, of the Institute for Medical Psychology in Munich. Many of its implications about the fundamental mechanism of beauty apply equally to the other neurocharms, but in some ways the charm of pattern is paradigmatic, and I do not wish to repeat myself more than necessary.

If human experimental subjects are shown simple visual images consisting of rows of vertical or horizontal lines, or lines diverging radially at equal angles from a point, they show a clear statistical preference for a certain frequency of lines. They prefer to look at a fairly rich field of lines, neither the simplest kind of row or star, made of only two or three lines, nor the densest kind, in which the lines are so close together they are indistinguishable, or so many that the eye loses track of them as individuals. In other words, the eye craves a certain complexity, but if the complexity is too great, and at the same time uniform, the eye reduces the pattern to a texture. The texture is now the only thing to look at, and so the eye finds itself as fatigued by the boredom of the single texture as it had been with a single line.

According to the same principle, subjects prefer images with more than one level of detail frequency, and with various kinds of texture; but again if the image is too "busy" and cannot be systematically organized into a hierarchy of detail-frequencies the eye becomes fatigued and generalizes the whole scene as a mishmash, which in turn, as such, produces visual boredom. If the image resolves itself into too simple a hierarchy, the eye—or rather the visual cortex—after an initial sensation of satisfaction at having solved the puzzle, begins to look about for ways in which the hierarchy either contains hidden contradictions or might be made to fit into a larger pattern. One example of a relatively complex and satisfying hierarchy is the perspective in which the world actually appears to us, its closer objects systematically larger than more distant ones, and its straight lines apparently curving in order to maintain the wholeness and consistency of the visual scene. It is interesting because such a scene implies occluded objects and spaces, which either invite investigative movement or speculation based on visible clues. It was in fact this richness of interpretive potential that served the great Renaissance masters of pictorial perspective.

One way of describing what is going on here is that boredom is our way of detecting inefficiencies and redundancies in a flow of information so that we are motivated to generalize repetitions as texture and concentrate on unique features of the visual scene. Those unique features include major contrasts, the borders between generalizable textures or tones, or structural outlines (which are two contrasts back to back). These then act as the higher-level signs or triggers or controls by which the lower-level information can be labeled, referred to, and retrieved.

The boredom response is in turn perhaps based on a universal characteristic of living cells, which makes every cell, however remote in function from the nervous system, a kind of neuron: that is, its capacity for irritation or sensitive response to stimulus, which can be overloaded and fatigued by the exhaustion of its capacity to respond, and habituated by repetition. If the eye is held still before a visual image, the image rapidly disappears, because the visual neurons are repeatedly and continuously getting the same stimulus. We are only able to see because the eye is free to range in a series of saccades, synchronized with the brain's alpha rhythm, and thus continually encounter new information. We do not see areas and states; we see contrasts and changes. This visual insistence on difference is emphasized by the fact that a given sector of the retinal field, tuned to fire if it receives a given stimulus, is always surrounded by a region in which sensitivity to that stimulus is actively suppressed. Interestingly enough, the area ratio of the receptive to the repressor field is almost exactly the golden section ratio.

The eye, then, tends to generalize if it can, to tag the ensemble of generalized elements (as a texture or a mishmash or a hierarchy) by means of a significant epitomizing fragment of it, to outline it with a contrast-boundary, to compress all that detail and push it down to lower-level processing, and then to look around for more interesting things to look at. Thus we can, with a scientific graph curve, generalize and smooth out its tendency, eliminating obvious mistakes and anomalies, and then extend and produce the curve in our imaginations, consistently with its existing trend. Or, to take a homelier example, an outfielder can judge the trajectory of a fly ball and be there when it arrives. Without the eye's activist policy of hierarchizing and generalizing visual information, we could not accomplish such feats. Certainly, this policy can produce mistakes; we can fail to take account of the crossing of critical thresholds in the graph, or of the gust of wind that catches the ball as it sails above the shelter of the bleachers. But next time we can include the new information as a parameter, and improve our odds of being right.

This, the default option of the optical system, consists in a sort of continuously correctable but deepening visual prejudice. There are other possible visual policies, such as those recommended by modernist aestheticians, which require us to abandon our prejudicial expectations and conventions, to treat every visual element as equally significant (or, which is the same thing, insignificant), and to avoid generalizations and visual hierarchies—especially those whose solution and meaning is the representation of a real object in space. But a species that relied on these would be unable to evade a falling rock or thrown spear, could not dance or make pictures, and would be blind to the beautifully intricate and coherent way in which the universe makes room for all its details, and reconciles all its forces and trajectories.

The great metallurgist and crystallographer Cyril Stanley Smith makes much the same point in his seminal essay "Structural Hierarchy in Science, Art, and History":

> Everything involves structural hierarchy; an alternation of external and internal, homogeneity and heterogeneity. Externally perceived quality (property) is dependent upon internal structure; nothing can be understood without looking not only at it in isolation on its own level but also at both its internal structure and the external relationships which simultaneously establish the larger structure and modify the smaller one. Most human misunderstanding arises less from differing points of view than from perceptions of different levels of significance. The world is a complex system and our understanding of it comes, in science, from the matching of model structures with the physical structure of matter and, in art, from a perceived relationship between its physical structure and the levels of sensual and imaginative perception that are possible within the structure of our brain's workings. All is pattern matching, with the misfits, if they can interact, forming a superstructure of their own as in moiré patterns or in beat notes. (Judith Wechsler, ed., *On Esthetics in Science* [Boston and Basel: Birkhauser Verlag, 1988], pp. 11–12)

Smith goes on to compare the various crystalline arrays that compose the phase structure of an alloy of brass with the beautiful textural arrays of an etching by a Japanese artist; and develops a fascinating theory of style based upon the emergent properties of dynamic hierarchical systems that are neither totally ordered nor totally disordered. We find a similar idea in Gerard Manley Hopkins's delightful Platonic dialogue on beauty, from which I shall quote at length. It begins with a discussion of the beauty of a chestnut fan, with its seven leaves and their complex gradations of size and complementary peculiarities of shape. The partners in the discussion agree that a six-leaved fan would not be so beautiful:

"I think the . . . odd-leaved one whatever its number of leaves, would be the handsomer; not, as you seem to shew, from the abstract excellence of an odd number, but because—well, I suppose because to have the greatest leaf in the middle is the handsomer way."

"But which is the more symmetrical?" asked the Professor. "Is not the six-leaved one?"

"Both have symmetry; yet, as you say, the six-leaved one seems the more so, supposing it of course to be really symmetrical, which this specimen is not."

"Is not this" asked the Professor "because it is naturally divided into two equal parts of three leaves each, while the seven-leaved is not, and cannot be symmetrical in the same way unless we physically cut the greatest leaf down the middle."

"Yes, that is it; I see" said Hanbury.

"And so you judge the less markedly symmetrical to be the handsomer. Still, the seven-leaved one has much symmetry. But now look at the tree from which I pulled it. Do you like it better as it is, or would you have the boughs start from the trunk at the same height on opposite sides, symmetrically pair and pair?"

"As it is, certainly."

"Or again look at the colouring of the sky."

"But" put in Hanbury "colouring is not a thing of symmetry."

"No; but now what is symmetry? Is it not regularity?"

"I should say, the greatest regularity" said Hanbury.

"So it is. But is it not that sort of regularity which is measured by length and breadth and thickness? Music for instance might be regular, but not symmetrical ever; is it not so?"

"Quite so" said Hanbury.

"Let us say regularity then. The sky, you see, is blue above, then comes a pale indescribable hue, and then the red of the sundown. You admire it do you not?"

"Very much" said Hanbury.

"But the red is the richest colour, is it not?"

"Now it is: yes."

"Should you then like the whole sky to be of one uniform rich red?"

"Certainly not."

"Or the red and blue to end sharply with a straight line, without anything as a gobetween?"

"No: I like the gradation."

"Again then you approve of variety over absolute uniformity. And variety is opposed to regularity, is it not? while uniformity is regularity. Is it not so?"

"Certainly. I am no doubt to conclude then that beauty is produced by irregularity" said Hanbury.

"Ah! you run on very fast" said the professor. "I never said that. . . . You will no doubt . . . see . . . that rows of level cloud run along the west of the sky."

". . . I can see them."

"Do you think they would be better away?" asked the Professor.

"No: they add to the beauty of the sunset sky."

"Notice however that they are pretty symmetrical. They are straight, and parallel with the sky-line and with each other, and of a uniform colour, and other things in them are symmetrical. Should you admire them more if they were shapeless?"

"I think not" said Hanbury.

"Again when we say anyone has regular features, do we mean praise or blame?"

"Praise."

"We were speaking of chestnut-trees, of their unsymmetrical growth. Now is the oak an unsymmetrical tree?"

"Very much so; O, quite a rugged boldly-irregular tree:

and this I should say was one of the things which make us invest it with certain qualities it has in poetry and in popular and national sentiment" said Hanbury. . . .

". . . Very good. Now have you ever noticed that when the oak has grown to its full stature uninfluenced, the outline of its head is drawn by a long curve, I should think it would be that of a parabola, which, if you look at the tree from a little way off, is of almost mathematical correctness?"

"Dear me, is it indeed so? No, I had never noticed it, but now that you name it, I do seem to find something in me which verifies what you say."

"Do you happen to remember" asked the Professor "that fine oak at the top of the hill above Elsfield where you have such a wide view?"

"Of course I do. Yes, a very fine tree."

"If you had analyzed your admiration of it I think you would have had to lay a great deal of it to that strict parabolic outline. Or again if one of the three side-leaves of this seven-leaved chestnut-fan be torn off, it will be less beautiful, will it not? And this, I am sure you will now say, because the symmetry is destroyed."

"Yes" said Hanbury. "Then beauty, you would say perhaps, is a mixture of regularity and irregularity." (W. H. Gardner, ed., *Poems and Prose of Gerard Manley Hopkins* [Harmondsworth: Penguin, 1953], pp. 94–97; my ellipses)

This close analysis of the beauty of visual pattern completes a set of ideas which, when we state them together, may be highly suggestive. Patterns are beautiful that exist at the margin between order and disorder, that exhibit a hierarchical organization which is troubled and opened up by contradictory elements. Those contradictory elements do not, however, obscure the hierarchy but add to it indeterminate metalevels which hold our visual interest and which are essentially dynamic and changing, so as to avoid the eye's tendency to become habituated or bored.

Only one kind of phenomenon can satisfy all these criteria, and that is the form of a growing organism or evolving system. Growth is a feedback process: an organism grows in proportion to its existing size and shape, and as an orderly continuation of its previous growth. The simplest kind of growth we know (as opposed to mere addition) is the Fibonacci series in mathematics, in which the next member of the series is simply the two previous members added together. Thus we get 1, 1, 2, 3, 5, 8, 13, 21, 34, 55, 89, etc. When this series is translated into a curve, we get the Fibonacci spiral, which is found throughout nature in the forms of growth, such as seashells and sunflower heads; I myself have measured the intervals between the fronds of a fern and found the series there too. If you try to make a spiral pattern by close-packing uniform elements (like sunflower seeds) outward from a center, you will always get just such a spiral. Leonardo Fibonacci discovered it as a way of calculating the theoretical rate of reproductive increase in a population of breeding rabbits.

This series is, interestingly enough, one of two ways in which the golden section ratio can be calculated; simply divide one member of the series by its successor. The further along the series one makes the calculation, the more accurate the value of the ratio will be. The other way of making the calculation is by taking the square root of 5, subtracting one, and dividing the result by two. This formula also has a spatial expression: take a regular five pointed star and calculate the ratio between the side of any of its points and the side of the pentagon that connects its internal angles. (This figure, the pentangle, pentacle, endless knot, or golden knot, is a traditional symbol of magic.) "Fiveness" is associated with the golden section in another way too: the "Penrose Tiling," by which the plane can be endlessly covered by a growing nonrepeating pattern made up of two shapes of parallelograms, continually suggests— without achieving—a fivefold symmetry: and the ratio of fat parallelograms to thin ones is the golden ratio. It is as if irregular growth is a spatial invention to replace for the regular pentagon the capacity to tile the plane regularly that is possessed by the other simple regular polygons—the triangles, squares, and hexagons.

Psychophysical experiments show that irrespective of culture and education, people prefer rectangles, the lengths of whose sides are related by the golden section ratio, to any other shape of rectangle. Thus the rudiments of visual beauty are founded upon the ratio of growth. The golden section is one of the core concepts in classical, medieval and Renaissance architecture and in the traditional visual arts.

But the Fibonacci series is only the simplest of a whole class of iterative algorithms or formulae whose results are fed back into the equation and which thus incorporate a mathematical feedback loop. Other examples include the Newtonian algorithm for obtaining square roots, the process by which such strange objects as Koch curves and Sierpinsky carpets are constructed, and the whole class of fractal algorithms described by Benoit Mandelbrot, including the Mandelbrot Set itself. (James Gleick's book *Chaos: Making a New Science* [New York: Viking, 1987] is a good lay introduction to this subject.) When the results of these iterative formulae are plotted in space, they produce exquisitely beautiful and elaborate forms, with depth below depth of detail at different hierarchical scalings; such forms please the eye, which recognizes in them the principles of animal, plant, and crystalline growth, and perhaps the principles of Growth itself. The attractors of Lorenz and Hénon, which plot the statistical results of a variety of natural iterative processes, share the same depth, clarity, and inexhaustible complexity; I believe the golden section can be found in many of their spatial relations.

Fractal theory is now used by computer graphics programs to store visual information with astonishing economy, as algorithmic seeds that need only to be played iteratively out to generate an accurate recreation of an original image. Thus computer programs, in the course of their hurried evolution, have discovered, as it were, the same techniques of generalizing, of compressing and pushing down, that the visual cortex did. We, and these new programs, do not remember by storing a picture but by storing just the essential inner information needed to recreate the picture: the algorithmic seed, or tag, or symbolic-metonymic epitome of the whole. We are thus in theory able to create a thousand pictures, by varying this algorithm, where a photographic memory could give us but one. This is the strategy not only of memory but of life, which does not hide its one talent in the ground, to be returned to its giver pure and unchanged; but which invests its being in a productive organic process that can not only copy over what it is given but produce new things that are not given.

The modernist denial of the shame of the organic made itself felt even in the realm of visual pattern. Bauhaus and, later, straight-edged minimalism replaced the flowing organic curves of Art Nouveau, which had in turn been a partial denial of the traditional biocultural forms of neoclassicism. Not that straight lines and linear simplicity are unbeautiful: their beauty consists in their re-minder of an organizing intelligence emerging from the flow of nature. But once the connection with nature is denied, then ugli-ness can result. The shapes of growth became in modernist visual arts the shameful reminder of a human beauty we had outgrown. There is a deep and sad irony in the idea of outgrowing growth.

Color. Color, as I have already suggested, is the next step down from texture in the brain's generalizing and hierarchizing process. The eye already interprets as color certain very fine textures, like rainbowy silk gauze moiré patterns, or the light-interference effects of bird feathers or moth pigment scales. How much richer color is, pushed down and generalized as it is, than it would be as texture or form, a conscious enumeration of wavelengths! This in itself is ample justification of the hierarchizing process. Like musical tone, color is a vast expressive language of its own that spans subjective experience, a neurobiological inheritance, and the natural world as a whole. Color is our visual way of tasting the world; it is our natural spectroscope, which tells us a great deal about the chemical constitution, surface structure, and energy state of other objects. And it is also a powerful means of communication and creation.

Victor Turner has profoundly analyzed the meaning of red, white, and black in Central African religious ritual and body paint-ing and has drawn provocative parallels with European and Ameri-can color symbolism. Red was bloodshed, menstruation, and life;

white was milk, sperm, and unearthly purity; and black was evil, filth, and death (but also the mystical darkness of revelation). There is a high degree of correspondence in the emotional tone of colors across the whole human race, a correspondence awkward to the imagination of our epoch. Part of the program of modernist relativism was based upon superficial but initially impressive cultural differences. For instance, white was often cited as the color of mourning in some Far Eastern societies, whereas black serves that function in the West. But as Herman Melville wisely pointed out in *Moby-Dick,* white is also a Western sign of death: the whiteness of shrouds, ghosts, candles, and sepulchers in our culture carries much the same feeling as the white robes of Japanese mourners. What is significant is that *one* of the achromatic tones was chosen as the sign of death in both culture areas; it is funereal *achromatism* that carries a large part of the universal affective charge.

Color used to be a favorite example for philosophers who wished to argue the linguistic contextuality of meaning. If they were correct, color names in different cultures should apply to different parts of the visible spectrum; what is a "pure" or "primary" color for one culture should be a "mixed" or "secondary" one for another. But superb cross–cultural research by Heinrich Zollinger and others has shown that all human beings see the same pure red, blue, yellow, and green at the same wavelength and saturation in the Munsell color space as we do, and name them accordingly. The mauves, violets, browns, magentas, chartreuses, and pinks occupy for other cultures the same more ambiguous place that they do for us, and the accuracy and consensus of the namers of such hues is correspondingly weaker.

The development of a specific abstract color vocabulary tends to follow the same path all over the world: first words for black and white appear, then red, then yellow or green, then blue, and so on; there are languages that have specific color words only for black and white, others that have only black, white, and red; but none that have words for brown or purple or pink without first having developed words for black, white, red, yellow, and so on. Of course in all languages there is a very accurate *metaphorical* color vocabulary, as we might use such terms as *banana-colored, blood-colored, grass-colored, aquamarine,* or *rose.* Not having a specific abstract word for a color, *contra* the cultural-linguistic determinists, does not mean that we cannot see it!

Color is immediately pleasurable, especially in combinations which, like musical tones, reflect the harmonic structure of the light spectrum in elegant ratios of wavelengths and wavelength combinations. This pleasure can be intensified in art, as the cognitive and active power of color is deepened in painting, mosaic, stained glass, and now photography and film.

Anyone who takes Wittgenstein's dictum "the limits of my language are the limits of my world" to mean that we are trapped within the preconceptions of words should spend a few minutes in front of a Van Gogh cornfield or a Gauguin Tahitian nude. Not, we might add, that one should wish to escape those linguistic preconceptions, despite the very theories of Impressionism that might invite such an escape. Van Gogh was a true artist, and the cornfield is the richer for the verbal meanings—of sacrament, of death's great recycling, of the terrible fullness of being—that we and the artist bring to it, and those meanings are in turn deepened by the painting. The cornfield is not exhausted but cultivated by them. And in Gauguin's masterpiece, *Where Did We Come From? What Are We? Where Are We Going?* the painter returns from the Rousseau-vian antimetaphysics of his times to the grand themes of shame, beauty, and emergent meaning.

But even color has its iconoclasts, who resent what they perceive as the shameful automatism of our pleasure in it. Perhaps, they suggest, color pleasure is kitsch. Perhaps we only enjoy color because the Foucauldian authorities dictate that we should, through the economies of mimetic desire, the dye science of the Industrial Revolution, the psychology of the voyeuristic gaze, and the hegemonic linguistic structures that underpin it all. This book is a challenge to that view in that it roots our pleasures in our very biology; but it is a biology generated by social and cultural reflexivities and feedbacks that are admittedly as unclean and shameful as the likes of Rousseau and Foucault evidently feel they are. But this book is also an invitation to accept the shame as the necessary precondition for beauty, and an assertion that the beauty is worth it.

Visual representation. The most complex and interesting kind of pattern, and the richest use of color, would naturally be connected with and include its own entire evolutionary history: that is, as well as being elegantly organized in itself, it would evoke and refer to the physical universe that generated it. It would, in other words, be some kind of picture. One of our most remarkable neurocharms is the ability of our bodies and brains to make recognizable pictures of the world. As I have already pointed out, we can by means of perspective include in a picture a synopsis of the universe itself, with the fascinating and open-ended suggestions provided by what perspectival occlusions must hide. By the narrativity inherent in pictorial representation we can add to the spatial dimensions of visual art the whole world of time, of that orderly temporal asymmetry and mysterious evolutionary potential that we find in story. When we use color as a description of objects, we can bring in the whole natural language of chemistry and physical luminance to deepen and ground the work of art.

An artist can of course choose not to use the extended vocabulary and magical power offered by this neurocharm and stick to the already rich language of pure pattern and color, with its emotional and spiritual connotations. Glorious works of abstract art have been composed under this self-imposed limitation; the "fascination of what's difficult" often leads the most accomplished artists to try what they can do, so to speak, with their left hands. By analogy, as a poet I have sometimes deliberately left out of a narrative poem the essential facts that would make it a proper story, or have included pieces of free verse in a metered poem. If, however, abstraction were the easy way out, a fashionable escape from the antique discipline of representation, as free verse has become the recourse of poets who do not know how to write in meter, then it would be a betrayal of art itself. Even the most severe of abstract art, if it is any good, cannot escape altogether the vitality of the actual living universe, and as we contemplate the abstract masterpieces they begin to become very deep pictures of things in the real world that we had not previously recognized—even when the artist's professed theory would deny any pictoriality. Again, by interrupting the neural world-construction process at some incomplete level, before representation has been fully achieved, they can show us how we see. Sometimes society has resisted and protested against such analysis; the art that endures such criticism is honored by it.

But picturing, of all the neurocharms, is perhaps the one that has aroused the greatest outpouring of anguished rage, the greatest feelings of shaming pollution. Judaism, Islam, the Byzantine Iconoclasts, the followers of Savonarola, and Puritan Christianity banned representation in whole or part. Modernist and postmodernist aesthetics were scarcely less repressive of pictoriality. Today there are new explosions over pornography and art. Here again, then, we find the encounter with the thrilling and terrible mystery of our evolved nature, with the sensitive membrane of our own bodily consciousness, to be more than we can bear; and too often our response has been denial, repression, and sometimes hysterical cruelty in defense of our denial. But here too is the strange shiver of beauty.

The prehistoric cave paintings at Lascaux and Altamira, and all over the world, are in a way the paradigm of our representational neurocharm. Their subject is the animal, that is, the sensitive (but victim) flesh recreated within the inner world of consciousness, sacrificed by being pictured. The vital life is thus controlled, celebrated, and commemorated, but kept hidden in the dark, in the burial place and holy ritual space of the tribe, where only by the promethean technology of fire, only on special ritual occasions, only for those persons who have the right, can the representational mystery be revealed.

Even in the very technique of visual representation, the essential shameful contradictions of our nature cannot be avoided. All representational painting and drawing and sculpting is a fantastic and unlikely compromise between conventional visual signs for objects—signs like the stick figure or smiling face or foursquare house of a child's drawing—and the photographic recording of retinal experience. That compromise is not between theory and reality, or between culture and nature, but between two levels of universal reality embodied in our neurogenetic makeup; which together and in their conflict find their most intense expression: nature always turning into self-reflection, self-reflection turning into nature. Picturing is only a more advanced form of the relationship between genetic code and living body.

Eight

The Last Five Neurocharms

DANCE. One of the most ancient neurocharms is our capacity to translate between the rhythms of music—the way we divide up time in such a way as to make it meaningful—and the spatially and visually significant gestures and movements of the body.

Dance is perhaps the most enduring, and freshest, image of the true nature of the universe. It reconciles individuality with unity, meaning with freedom. In it the human body becomes a living image of the cosmos as a whole. Artists, theologians, and scientists are unanimous in describing the world as a dance: Christian Shakers, Muslim Whirling Dervishes, and Jewish Hasids dance to become one with God. Across the human race dance is central to puberty initiations, courtship, weddings, welcome ceremonies, work rituals, vegetation and fertility rituals, astronomical celebrations, hunting, battle mimes and moriscas, curing rituals, funerals, ecstatic and mystical rites, and clowning. The experience of dance, both for participant and audience, is one in which we rediscover our whole evolutionary history as physical organisms, the pumping of blood and air, the intricate innervation of muscle and internal organs, the sheer excitement of conscious controlled spontaneous movement.

This neurocharm builds upon the general mammalian vocabulary of body language and is also deeply connected with the martial arts and with sports. It had utilitarian aspects in such cooperative, kinetic, and complexly rhythmic activities as warfare and hunting, but I believe its main evolutionary boost came, like the other charms, from ritual. It was not so much that ritual dance grew out of fighting as that the human ways of fighting grew out of ritual dance.

In the traditional Oriental martial arts, such as tai-chi, karate, and kendo (the art of the sword), the ancient connection between the dance of combat and the spiritual values of purity, insight, and contemplation was never lost. It was evidently present in the ancient Greek fighting arts, and the spiritual importance of gymnastics and wrestling are attested by Greek sculpture, by the funeral and celebratory games of Homeric epic, and by the educational theory of Plato's *Republic*. Renaissance Italian fencing theory is full of concepts and terms from music and dance and has fine theories about breathing and spiritual preparation.

Some theorists of the Eastern martial arts have suggested that Alexander's armies might have brought Greek wrestling, boxing, and weapons arts to India, that like Buddhism the techniques were then carried to China over the Himalayas, and that karate might thus be an heir of those games Pindar sang of in Greece. But I have seen African hunter's dances that show a similar empirical and spiritual understanding of the power centers of the body, the importance of the breath, and the rhythmic foundations of effective and expressive movement; and I have been present at Plains Indian powwows where I saw the same things. This neurocharm did not need cultural diffusion to appear all over the world; it is wired in, like the others.

Modern and postmodern aesthetic theory has tended to separate dance from religion, sports, and the martial arts, for reasons that will be familiar. Some of the old truths are now being rediscovered by sports medicine and sports psychology, and one hears often of basketball players and football running backs getting ballet or meditation training; some of the fragmented parts of this old ritual are coming back together. John MacAloon argues that the Olympic Games are a panhuman ritual whose central sacrament is the body. Perhaps its revival came just in time for the human race.

Ideographics. This charm forms the essential link between the right-brain picturing ability and the left-brain linguistic ability, as poetic meter does between right-brain music and left-brain language. Without these connecting neurocharms, perhaps, the miraculous knot of human ritual might never have been tied together in such a way that it could itself culturally evolve and in turn drive the biological evolution of the species. Jacques Derrida is right in his insight that "writing" is not a late and inauthentic addition to an originally oral world (though he is of course wrong in reducing everything else to writing). Visual representations of verbal ideas are culturally universal; it is clear from the earliest records we have of human activities, signs scratched on bone or stone, that we were ideographists as far back as we can tell.

In mathematics we find the ideographic muse in that most fertile connection between geometry and algebra. Once geometry becomes thus linked to logic and trope, an extraordinarily sturdy system of thought and discovery emerges in which the limitations of the verbal symbolizing power are compensated for by the instantaneous gestalts of visual pattern-recognition, and vice versa. Out of this realm also comes much of the underpinning of architecture, the pleasures of design and sculpted space, and the whole rich and powerful technique of maps, charts, graphs, and diagrams. The most powerful neurochemical rewards seem to be associated with the difficult passage and translation of concepts and experiences across the corpus callosum that connects the two hemispheres of the brain. That passage is almost synonymous with insight.

The new graphics abilities that our cybernetic technology has given us, to represent any kind of information in striking visual ways, are a natural extension of this neurocharm. We are superimposing upon normal physical space a second universal medium, which some have called cyberspace. Like Chinese landscape painting, its shapes will be suggestive of ideographs, and its ideographs will be a continuation of nature's own shaping; like the memory theaters of the Renaissance, it will be a place to collect the present, to recollect the past, and to adaptively select the future.

Poetic meter. In an earlier book, *Natural Classicism,* I reported at length the research on this neurocharm that the distinguished Munich psychophysicist Ernst Pöppel and I conducted during the last two decades. I shall only summarize it here, but it was the discoveries we made, especially the extraordinary correspondences between the findings of neuroscience, traditional poetic practice, worldwide anthropological evidence, and close literary research and analysis, that really convinced me of the existence and importance of the neurocharms in general.

Poetic meter mediates between left-brain linguistic capacities and right-brain musical and gestalt capacities. All over the world human beings compose and recite poetry in poetic meter; all over the world the meter has a line-length of about three seconds, stretching sometimes to about four and a half for solemn poetry, and contracting sometimes to as little as two for comic poetry.

The three-second line, we found to our excitement, was tuned to the three-second information processing cycle in the human brain, which Pöppel was investigating in his laboratory. Our aware mental present is three seconds long—we remember echoically and completely three seconds' worth of information, before it is passed on to a longer-term memory system, where it is drastically edited, organized for significant content, and pushed down to a less immediate level of consciousness. Thus poetic meter is the most efficient and memorable way of communicating verbal information.

If a natural brain rhythm, like the ten-cycle-per-second alpha rhythm, is "driven" or amplified by an external rhythmic stimulus, the result can be large changes in brain state and brain chemistry; in the case of the alpha rhythm, epilepticlike seizures. The effect of driving the three-second cycle is much more benign and has been investigated in the study of chant-induced ritual trance. Chanting the same three-second phrase over and over again, or different three-second phrases with identical rhythmic structure, can produce changes in brain chemistry, and consequently in the amount and kind of information that the brain can absorb, and in the kind of higher-level processing it can put to work. A state resembling the relaxed awareness that is the goal of meditative disciplines is attained, but at the same time a powerful channel is opened up between the linguistic left temporal lobe of the brain, normally somewhat isolated, and the emotive and evocative limbic system. New experiences of insight and empathy with nature and with other human beings become possible.

But poetry takes this basic cycle and builds on it (much as our genetically based rituals must have been transformed by new, culturally evolved traditions). The poetic line is shaped according to a repeated pattern of feet or other subunits, whose elements are syllables that differ as to length, stress, or, in tonal languages like Chinese, tone. Against this pattern significant and expressive variations can be played. For instance, the English iambic pattern consists of a regular pulse of one unstressed and one stressed syllable (thus: ˘ ´). But consider this sonnet by Shakespeare (18), which is based on the same iambic (˘ ´) pattern of syllables, yet varies freely on it without losing touch with it:

> Sháll Ĭ cŏmpáre thĕe tŏ ă súmmĕr's dáy?
> Thóu ărt móre lŏvelў ănd mŏre témpĕrăte.
> Róugh winds dŏ shăke thĕ dárliňg buds ŏf Máy,
> Aňd súmmĕr's léase hăth áll tóo short ă dáte.
> Sómetíme tóo hŏt thĕ éye ŏf héavĕn shínes,
> Aňd óftĕn ĭs hĭs góld cŏmpléxiŏn dímmed;
> Aňd évĕrў fáir frŏm fáir sŏmetímes dĕclínes,
> Bў chánce, ŏr nătúre's chángiňg cóurse, ŭntrímmed;
> Bŭt thў étĕrnăl súmmĕr shăll nŏt fáde,
> Nŏr lóse pŏsséssiŏn ŏf thát fáir thŏu ów'st,
> Nŏr shăll Déath brág thŏu wănd'rĕst ĭn hĭs sháde,
> Whĕn ĭn étĕrnăl línes tŏ tíme thŏu gŕow'st.
> Sŏ lóng ăs mén căn bréathe, ŏr éyes căn sée,
> Sŏ lóng líves thĭs, ănd thĭs gíves lĭfe tŏ thĕe.

The difference between the expected rhythm and the actual rhythm carries information, as a tune does, or as a line does in a drawing; and that information is processed and understood not with the linguistic left brain but with the musical and spatial right brain. Thus unlike ordinary language, poetic language comes to us in a "stereo" neural mode, so to speak, and is capable of conveying feelings and ideas that are usually labeled nonverbal; the genre itself is a biocultural feedback loop that makes us able to use much more of our brain than we normally can. The protean quality of poetic meter allows it to draw in to the same artistic work a variety of other neurocharms, including the metaphysical-speculative, the troping-symbolical, the ideographic-architectonic, the narrative, the power of dramatic mimesis, and of course, through song, the somewhat different aptitudes of musical meter.

Poetic meter, however, carries with it the full shame of our evolutionary roots, in its evocation of nursery rhyme and sacrificial chant, its arousal of the vulnerable old sweetness I have imaged in the girl with her mother's dress. Moreover, like several other charms, poetic meter requires considerable training in its mastery, and thus the neophyte is exposed to the shame of incapacity as part of the initiation into full participation. Since shame was for the moderns the worst of all evils, poetic meter came to be abhorred and associated with a blush of disgust at rhymes and jingles and with the embarrassing mother figure lampooned in the caricature of the blue-haired trinominate lady poet. Free verse, with its antiseptic safety, was substituted. We see this psychological move clearly in the career of William Carlos Williams. There were, indeed, legitimate artistic reasons for profound metrical experiment, which inspired the extraordinary variations on the traditional forms that we find in the work of Pound and Eliot. But a generation of poets grew up who had lost touch with their ancient shamanic brothers and sisters and did not know what they had missed. Now another generation has come that must seek painfully in the realms of the dead for the beauty and the shame that was lost.

Cuisine. The human brain is like an ancient sacred text that has been added to over millennia, transformed, partially edited, and conflated with its own heavy and repeated marginal interpretation, scholia, and allegorical glosses. The evolutionary rewiring of the brain transformed the archaic olfactory bulb and its attachments into the limbic system, making it, as Jonathan Winson has shown, the gateway of memory and the source of emotion and motivation. Perhaps reflecting the archaic dependence of sexual arousal and maturation upon the sense of smell, the limbic system, through its hypothalamic connection to the pituitary, is also the controller of the hormone system of the body. A further close connection exists with the pineal structure, which is the remnant of a third eye among our ancient premammalian ancestors; evidently the diurnal and annual cycles of light and darkness helped set the clock of the reproductive system.

This whole complex was then adapted as the basis of the complex affective life of the higher mammals. The new associative cortex, which is the carrier of human consciousness, reflection, and reason, is in a sense a cortical outgrowth of that limbic complex. This evolutionary process had the peculiar effect of leaving the sense of smell, and thus a large part of the sense of taste, directly connected to memory, emotion, and to the higher associative functions, but with almost no connection to the linguistic centers of the left temporal lobe. Hence smells and tastes are immensely evocative and memorable, and are, like Proust's madeleine cake, central to our emotional and intellectual lives; but we often cannot put a name to them.

However, the touch sensitivity and proprioceptive motor skills of the tongue, mouth, and palate, that we require for the production of speech, and which *are* closely connected to the linguistic centers, are also available for the appreciation of the tactile and mechanical properties of food; we can taste and savor the texture of words. Thus the various elements of cuisine are related by very different brain structures and functions; and the neuroanatomical history of cuisine becomes a fascinating comment on the nature of this important neurocharm.

Animals eat; humans dine. As Claude Lévi-Strauss points out, human beings all over the world use the distinction between the raw and the cooked to express the essence of the distinction between nature and culture. The French *cru,* for "raw," is the root of our word *crude;* crude oil, the foundation of our economy, must be cracked for its volatiles in a "refinery." But the myths Lévi-Strauss analyzes do not so much distinguish between nature and culture as show culture to be a special, tricky, active, self-reflective *part* of nature. Nature gives birth to culture, and as nature *means* giving birth (as in "nativity"), then culture is nature squared, multiplied by itself, re-naissance. As we recall from the myths of Sedna and Prometheus, the transgression that cooks the world is the most characteristically selved and alive part of nature. The fingers of Sedna that her father cuts off become the marine mammals, the food of the Inuit; the fire Prometheus steals, which human beings will use for cooking and sacrifice, is the gods' own fire.

The division of the spoils of the hunt, and the sacrifice of that moiety of it which is reserved to the gods (who permit us first to substitute metaphorically the animal's death for the human's, and then, synecdochically, to substitute part of the animal for the whole), is followed by the ritual banquet. And the banquet is the place where most of the other great neurocharms can be brought together in a celebration of our humanity: song and dance, metered storytelling, the plastic and performative mimesis of the mysteries, divination (sometimes by the sacrificial entrails), metaphysical and symbolic interpretation.

The Passover, with its special, evocative herbs, its sacrificial lamb, and its unleavened bread and wine, is a commemoration of the liberation of humankind from the bondage of mere animality, the irreversible historical evolution of the people into self-awareness, the substitution of circumcision and the blood smeared on the lintels for the death of the firstborn. It is structured around a series of questions that establish the primal lexicon of human meaning; and it encounters squarely the shame of the young who must ask the questions because they do not know. But that shame is transformed into a strange, familiar beauty, an evocativeness that can bring tears to the eyes. Likewise, the eucharist celebrates the most shameful fact of all, which is that we sacrifice and eat the body of God as indeed we eat the bodies of all our ancestors; but it is all commuted into the Word and thus redeemed. "In other words," this sacrificial meal, this sacrament, is the place where meaning is generated; it celebrates the transubstantiation in the gut of dead matter into living spirit, and, in the spirit, of the literal into the figurative, the existential into the meaningful. The soul-food banquets of every human community repeat these themes with infinite variations.

As with the other neurocharms, the human creative imagination has woven the ancient ritual capacities of the feast into a rich and swiftly evolving art of its own. In France and China especially, cuisine shows the hallmarks of the great natural classical genres. It is infinitely generative without losing its thematic unity, a unity based in France on wheat grain, milk, olive oil, the egg and the grape, and in China on rice, the bean, and the oils of certain nuts and seeds. It unites the loftiest metaphysical and medical theory with an expert practical knowledge of human pleasure. And it is deeply rooted in the imaginative life of the people, in the seasons, the life-crises, childhood, and close kinship.

But behind the joy of the feast there is always a death and a pollution; and, as Edwin Watkins points out, a division of the *moirai,* or cuts of the prey, according to the merit and status of the guests. When merit and status conflict, there is a *neikos,* or brawl, over the possession of the body of the prey or of the dead hero, a struggle that is at the core of tragic action. If this division is acknowledged and accepted, it becomes the foundation of human society, but if it is contested it leads to the potential violation of the social bond and the breaking of the round table. The dark and shameful side of the feast appears in our most basic sensory and emotional vocabulary. Used food, shit, is the foulest thing we know. The words *host, guest,* and *hostile* all come from the same root, and the German cognate of the English word *gift* means "poison." Lucre, or money, is filthy precisely because it reminds us of the shameful conflict between justice and equality in the division of the spoils. To dine "high on the hog" is to have a better portion in life.

The most shameful action we can perform is to give a bad gift; and tragically that is the first gift we make, the gift of a baby's freshly created turd, warm from its own body, to its mother in thanks for its own birth and existence. The rest of life is the search for an acceptable substitute gift; a search that is the tragedy of existence and the source both of our wisdom and of our miraculous sense of humor. We live through the death of others, and this is simply the datum of our existence. In traditional societies the pollution attendant on eating is acknowledged, and the ritual of the banquet turns the shame to beauty; but what if we were to lose that ritual and deny the pollution?

We can observe in the food taboos of this century, and to some extent the last, the same movement to deny shame that we have seen elsewhere. Our century, let us say at once, is not unique in having food taboos. Indeed, most traditional religious employ food taboos as an explicit way of symbolically distinguishing our reflective and human lives from the material and animal existence out of which we came, and of distinguishing "us," the chosen and enlightened, from "them," the tribes of the infidels. This is a central meaning of the Passover, to name but one major food taboo ritual. Strict food laws, including in some cases vegetarianism, are found in traditional Catholicism, Islam, Hinduism, and Buddhism. However, these ritual prohibitions affirm our humanity while accepting the inevitable shame and pollution of our condition.

Contemporary food taboos have a rather different flavor, which is extremely complex. The contemporary eater must thread a minefield of uncomfortable categories; it is no wonder that many of us, especially children, are almost pathologically finicky, and that eating disorders such as anorexia and bulimia abound. The ideological advocacy of whole food and health food ("whole" and "health" share etymological roots with *holy*) often amounts to a kind of denial of cookery, a denial of our humanity, and it is sometimes, as with the bran fad, a sign of virtue if the result is pleasureless and tasteless. Modern ideological vegetarianism seeks to erase the distinction between humanity and the rest of nature, while at the same time denying our actual kinship with the animal world. It implicitly asserts that nature is static and nonevolutionary, and that any innovation in it, such as human ideas and activities, is a sort of disease or cancer. It is a rejection of the carnivorous gusto of our animal nature; it hates the stink of meat.

"Natural" food is ideally food that is not cooked, that does not claim a special place for human beings; but at the same time it implies disdain for the bestiality of more traditional eaters. Politically the cardinal sin has become "greed"; not, it might be noted, avarice or miserliness, which would better fit the socioeconomic theory. One's political enemies are called "pigs."

All this is not to deny the delicious and nutritious qualities of fresh and unprocessed ingredients. Nor is it to defend the diet of the industrialized West, which, because of affluence and technology, has been able to supply the consumer every day with what once would have been the foods only of ceremonial and special occasions—meats and sweetmeats, fatty roasts, rich creamy desserts, wines and spirits. But in our eagerness to escape the shame of our condition we have sometimes forgotten the wisdom of Falstaff and Sir Toby Belch, Shakespeare's heroes of the feast: "If sack and sugar be a fault, God help the wicked! If to be old and merry be a sin, then many an old host that I know is damned. If to be fat is to be hated, then Pharaoh's lean kine are to be loved" (*1 Henry IV* 2.4.475). "Dost thou think, because thou art virtuous, there shall be no more cakes and ale?" (*Twelfth Night* 2.3.116).

Despite the attacks upon it, cuisine as an art is alive and well. Somehow the bourgeoisie has been able to take on the mantle of patronage from the aristocracy without the arguable losses in quality that have befallen some of the other arts. Wines and cheeses, say the critics, have never been better. Even in the gastronomically dull regions of Germany, Britain, and America the quality of food has improved enormously. In America, especially, we see the rise of remarkable new cuisines, based on an amplification of traditional regional themes (Tex-Mex, Pennsylvania Dutch, Southern, Cajun, New England coast) by exposure to French, Italian, Indian, and East Asian cooking. The theory of beauty that this book develops would offer various suggestions. Cuisine should not lose touch with its roots in childhood, peasant, ceremonial and soul food (*Nouvelle Cuisine* is perhaps too pure). It should, however, seek greater unity with the other arts. It should pay attention to the emotional, mnemonic, and evocative connections of the sense of smell. And it should explore the poetry of texture (especially well developed in Chinese cooking, perhaps because of its strong Taoistic element) which is so closely involved with speech.

Massage. This neurocharm is still largely undeveloped as an art in the West and exhibits the cultural features that might have been found in painting and music before they were recognized as arts, their rules discovered, and their practitioners remembered by name. Yet it has a potent evolutionary base. Grooming is perhaps the most important of all rituals in many primate species, and a sensitive and neurally sophisticated tactile interpretation-action system is involved in many of our most basic activities: wrestling, lovemaking, sculpture and ceramics, dance, infant care, the taming and training of animals, and, most developed of all, medical diagnosis and therapy. The laying-on of hands, the gentling of animals and children, and the arts of love alike require a strange and special insight, and can be so beautiful in their effect that they raise the hair upon one's nape. In some Asian societies there is a body of theory associated with this neurocharm, recorded in such works as the *Kama Sutra* and the Chinese and Japanese scholarly texts of acupressure, hand- and foot-massage, and acupuncture. In the West there is a tradition of empirical expertise in massage and chiropractic, partly handed down from the ancient Greeks and Romans, and more recently, perhaps via the crusades, from the Egyptians and Turks.

With the modernist attempt to separate sex from any shaming entanglements with the rest of human life, there was an upsurge of interest in the technical aspects of sexual intercourse, but the approach was doomed to failure as an art precisely because it denied shame. There is a sort of one-shot pleasure in the destruction of a given shame-barrier, for instance the traditional concealment of a certain part of the body or a traditional reticence in gender behavior; but if that shame is abolished (rather than being violated, acknowledged, and reaffirmed) it ceases to exist as a source of pleasure and some much harder, rougher, and more explicit shamelessness is then required to extract an equivalent amount of pleasure. Sex used in this way resembles the process of addiction to a drug, in which habituation dulls the receptors and demands larger and larger doses.

The true art of sexual love involves not a liquidation of the sources of shame but their elaboration from mere social stereotypes into the most complex and individual psychospiritual labyrinths, delays, and trompes l'oeil. For first, virgin lovers, abstinence, honor, chastity and sublimation can often carry more of the true sexual charge, a pleasure disseminated and immanent in every act of life and every experience, than any rush to the "master and main exercise, th'incorporate conclusion," as Shakespeare's Iago nastily puts it. And older, faithfully married lovers find more, perhaps, in some nuance of tender irony, intimate politeness, or acceptance of mortality, than the promiscuous and sexually athletic can know. We need only consult Rembrandt's pictures of Saskia to be aware of this.

The problem with the tactile neurocharm is that until now there were few ways of separating tactile art from tactile reality, of representing or pretending or miming or recording touch so that it can be artistically played with and experimented on and enriched by virtual and hypothetical dimensions. But touch and proprioception may have an extraordinary future as an art form, now that we have begun to develop kinesthetic and tactile technology and a virtual space, called cyberspace, to play in. We can already see the dim beginnings of such an art in computer videogames, dungeons-and-dragons, role-playing games, Disneyland rides, aviation and military simulation software, Civil War battle re-enactments, and remote pressure-sensing and manipulation technology. New piezoelectric materials and recording devices, and sophisticated robotic-human interfaces, are opening up the field. And already remote sensing gloves and whole-body suits which give the illusion of being in another place are being developed.

If we can transfer our mysterious neural body into another space or time, where the physical—and moral—rules are different, and experience and act in the person of a software construct in a cyberspace world, or of a remote-controlled dummy in the real world, the artistic possibilities are endless. No doubt the immediate uses of this technology will be practical, and then crude war games and pornographic scenarios will be tried out. What would be the moral status of killing, in the person of one's own construct, the person of your enemy's construct? What about the morality of a simulated affair with your neighbor's spouse, both using simulated bodies?

The issues here immediately begin to spill over into those of art. What kind of theater might be possible with an audience wired into the actors' physical experience? What new forms of dance might be possible in cyberworlds with different gravitational characteristics, or in virtual-reality body constructs with different muscular structures and powers, or different senses and organs than the human? What if we could fly in such a world? What would it be like to see in ultraviolet, or infrared, or radio waves? What imaginary architectures, or adventures, or animals, or civilizations? After such a technology had been in use for some hundreds of years, and the worlds of the past recorded kinetically as well as in the senses of sight, hearing, smell, and taste, might one not then be able to enter the past and replay great events, or even one's own childhood? And what would fictions consist of in such a world?

Any discussion of the tactile neurocharm would be incomplete without a mention of tickling. Tickling, and the laughter that it engenders, is our closest physical synecdoche for the general relationship of shame and beauty. We cannot tickle ourselves, but to be tickled is to be most aware of self. Tickling is the fleshly experience of shame: unbearable without laughter, which is the fleshly experience of beauty. The release of orgasm is often associated with laughter, transforming shame into epiphanic joy. And laughter, elaborated into comedy and the sense of humor, is perhaps a super-neurocharm of its own, designed to recognize and transcend the dissonances within and between all the other neurocharms.

Nine

Beauty and the Anima Mundi

W HEN WE consider the contemporary natural and human sciences as a whole, what emerges is a remarkable vision of the universe and its history. This vision will, I believe, serve the same function with respect to twenty-first century humanity that the Great Chain of Being did for the High Middle Ages and the Renaissance: a way of connecting cosmos and psyche, of ascertaining and generating value, and of guiding creative action and innovation. The terrible events of this century have, I believe, left a sufficient residue of poisons in our intellectual and artistic culture—despair, denial, and distortion—so that this new vision will have a very difficult time coming into the world. But it is the only one that now offers any intellectual space for play, for a loving acceptance of ourselves and of the rest of nature, for creative research, and for really new art, and so I believe that the human imagination and the "holiness of the heart's affections" will not long be able to resist its temptations.

Though the comparison with the Great Chain of Being is a valid one in some ways, there are immense differences between the emerging new synthesis and the old. First, and most important, the new synthesis is essentially dynamic, changing, evolutionary, historical, and irreversible, while the old was static, unchanging, creationist, eternal, and cyclic in its temporal manifestation. In the new synthesis (which we might as well call the evolutionary synthesis) new realities—new species, for instance—can emerge, whereas in the old Aristotelian-Thomistic system species, or kinds of things living or unliving, are eternal categories, which their temporal exemplars or avatars in the material world strive without full success to fulfill and accomplish.

The second major difference is that the old synthesis works through a fundamentally top-down causality and ordering process, whereas the new synthesis, at least in its early stages, is largely bottom-up in its causality and ordering. In the Thomist universe God created and ruled the angels and human beings, who themselves ruled over the animals, which in turn were given domain over the plants, which controlled their inanimate material food, and so on down. In the evolutionary universe the sequence is reversed: the laws and particles of physics largely determine the ground rules of chemistry, which provides the arena for life, which in turn produces and generates conscious minds.

Of course in the Thomist universe things did not necessarily go according to the ideal pattern, because of free will, the differences between matter and spirit, and the disordered attempt of lower organisms to usurp a higher place. And in the new synthesis, bottom-up material determinism, operating through the variative-selective process of evolution, paradoxically brings about organisms which, as wholes, determine themselves and their inner and outer environment as much as or more than they are themselves determined. Thus in the new synthesis a top-down, whole-to-part creative ordering can exist, though it must first be brought into the world, and must continually be maintained, by a bottom-up, part-to-whole evolutionary or metabolic process. Together, then, in the evolved state of the world, bottom-up and top-down causality cooperate in a complex feedback system that is capable of further self-elaboration into yet more reflexive states of being.

The last major difference between the old Great Chain of Being and the new evolutionary universe is that whereas the former requires an outside creator and arranger, the former is self-creating and self-organizing. The old worldview provides an eternal transcendent God radically separated and distinguished from his creations by the fact that he alone is self-sufficient and self-creating. The new view, on the other hand, is approaching the position that the universe is a logical necessity; that is, the existence of a state of affairs in which nothing at all existed would require some extraordinary, ineffable, and transcendent metaphysical intervention; but the existence of an evolving, self-organizing universe is essentially inevitable without such an intervention.

This view places the characteristics of loving fruitfulness, the apparent intention of design, and teleology, once postulated as necessarily belonging to the creator, in the creation itself, if they are anywhere at all. Until a couple of decades ago it was assumed that the physical universe works deterministically, and so if we accepted the new view we were forced to assume that those "creatorly" characteristics were nonexistent, illusions imposed upon a blind and automatic universe by our animistic expectations. In other words our intellectual honesty required us to disbelieve our eyes and ears, which told us of the joy of creation as it sings itself into being. But now the new mathematics, physics, and chemistry of nonlinear nondeterministic dynamical systems show us that the physical universe is, in effect, free, and can thus be held responsible for its own beautiful order, richness, and creative innovation.

There is an apparent contradiction between the idea that the universe *had* to come into existence and that it is free. But this contradiction is only apparent. *Some* kind of evolving, self-organizing universe is a necessity; but which one it is, how it evolves, which directions it takes are, so to speak, up to its own choice. And *choice* is really not a bad word at all to describe the way in which, as the new science has shown, complex and unstable dynamical systems, on the verge of some transformation and unable to hold their present arrangement intact (for instance, a hot but cooling universe of pure energy about to give birth to matter, or a supersaturated crystalline solution, or an ecosystem with more resources at its disposal than it is using, or a heart between beats) unpredictably "collapse" into one of a large number of possible new states. The collapse is unpredictable, not necessarily because any of its contributing elements are disordered, but because all of them are dependent on each other in a complex contextual feedback relationship and must thus all change together, without a causal priority and sequence that can be analyzed by any system smaller than the universe itself. The fact that this new state will fall within the parameters of a very beautiful and elaborate "strange attractor," and not outside it, is an indication not of the *lack* of choice in this sense, but of its orderly coherency, its nonrandomness.

The current evolutionary vision of the world, which, now that we have qualified the meaning of the phrase, we might call the Great Tree of Being, needs a brief general summary here. Scientists, who for the most part are at work upon some small section of it, often do not pay much attention to the shape of the whole; though there are exceptions, such as Roger Penrose, Roald Hoffman, J. T. Fraser, Stephen Hawking, Paul Davies, John Archibald Wheeler, Lynn Margulis, Roger Sperry, and George Seielstadt, among others. Scholars in the humanities often have an idea of science based more upon the philosophy of science than on contemporary developments in science itself, a philosophy of science in turn based upon or critiquing scientific ideas that are over half a century old.

Large areas of the new vision are still under vigorous debate; for instance, many environmental and ecological scientists are inclined, because of the synchronic and synergetic nature of their subject, to ignore or deny the differences in level of anatomical and functional development between species and interpret the interdependence of different species as equality. Evolutionary biologists, anatomists, organ specialists, ethologists, and neuroscientists, on the other hand, are usually so close to the miraculous specializations and hierarchy of biological function in the organisms they study, and to the evolutionary history through which the less organized developed into the more organized, that the terms *higher functions, higher organisms, more advanced species,* and so on are fundamental to their work and implicit in the nature of things. For the former, a virus or bacterium is in theory just as valuable as a mammal, even as a human being. For the latter, the greater complexity of higher organisms makes them more interesting, more wonderful, and more important to preserve than their less-evolved kin, though even the lowest living organism is a miracle compared with a piece of nonliving matter.

Nevertheless such debates, except where exacerbated by ideological hatred and political manipulation within an ignorant public domain, are capable of resolution through a more sophisticated consideration of different perspectives. Certainly for the purposes of a forest ecologist, a virus, which may only be a tiny clipping of RNA with no metabolic machinery of its own, that must parasitize the cellular infrastructure of some plant's leaf to exist at all, may be just as crucial a part of an ecosystem as an oak or a moose (or a human tribesman or woman). Meanwhile, for a paleobiologist or cytobiologist such a virus would be only a living fossil of an age of biological complexity infinitely more primitive than that of the moose's least muscle cell, whose smallest gene would be more subtle in operation and function. We see things differently with a microscope than with a telescope.

But the two viewpoints are not irreconcilable; in fact they are complementary results of a self-consistent whole, given the biologically based mental system in which we generalize, symbolize, compress, and push down to a lower level of attention any information that we receive—ironically, a hierarchizing process in itself. Moreover, both the ecologist and the evolutionary biologist would recognize a difference in complexity and organization between a live organism and a dead one, and would be much less interested in the latter. A chemist or physicist might prefer to work with nonliving matter and resent the pro-life prejudices of the biologists. So the argument is not one that denies relative value, but differs, because of professional perspective, on where it should be laid.

Given these qualifications, what does our new Great Chain or Tree of Being look like? The most exciting mathematical ideas of our century deal with the incompleteness and open-endedness of any mathematical system and its propensity to generate paradoxes that can only be resolved in terms of some richer and more reflexive system that induces it—a system that must in turn contain its own paradoxes, and so on. These relationships, of inclusion, containment, open-endedness, incompleteness, extension, betweenness, and even, as in the case of the orientation of the imaginary number series with respect to the real numbers, orthogonality and thus angles—immediately suggest spacelike dimensions. The discipline of topology may be defined as a demonstration that space, spatial dimensionality, is the only solution to certain problems in mathematical logic. Space is the way that true statements that would contradict each other if they were in the same place, space themselves out from each other. The Pauli exclusion principle, which states that two identical particles cannot occupy the same energy-state at the same place and time, is a physical example of this idea. If the two particles were in the same place, they would be both two and one, which violates the noncontradiction law of logic. In other words, a nonspatial world, if everything thinkable within it is to remain logically consistent, must necessarily generate a spatial world.

The new fractal geometry includes a working concept of how a given dimension can be generated and coherent definitions of partial dimensions. We are familiar in classical geometry with zero-dimensional points, one-dimensional lines, two-dimensional planes, three-dimensional volumes, and so on; popular science has invited us to imagine more dimensions still. But the noninteger dimensions of fractal mathematics—a given curve can have a dimensionality of 1.62, for instance—are a new concept and show us how we might, through the feedback of an iterative algorithm, actually get from one integer dimension to another.

Certain other problems in mathematics involve the relative easiness or difficulty of a calculation. Some calculations wind themselves up without complication. Others involve more and more subcalculations, and sub-subcalculations, before the calculator can produce an answer. In order to be able to talk coherently about such distinctions, and to measure their differences, we need another kind of dimensionality: time. In its simplest form time is to the three spatial dimensions what the imaginary number series—the square roots of the negative numbers—is to the real number series. Time gives us a dimension within which we can describe the difficulty of a calculation, whether it is soluble in an amount of time that increases polynomially with the number of variables in it, or exponentially, or more swiftly still, or infinitely; and if infinitely, which of Cantor's larger and larger infinities it would be.

Thus space-time emerges out of very logic; and given space-time, theoretical and cosmological physics can show the necessity of the Big Bang, of the emergence of energy as the coherent solution of certain possible and necessary space-time geometrical paradoxes, and of the self-binding collapse of energy into matter as the universe cools with its expansion. Matter is the solution to paradoxes that arise in the energy universe as the primal superforce separated itself out into gravitation, electromagnetism, the weak and the strong nuclear forces.

We might add that not every possible kind of energy and matter does emerge, and once having emerged, survive; there are apparently no magnetic monopoles, though there could have been; and there is very little antimatter, since at the point of the collapse into matter, physical laws demanded that the energy universe choose one or the other but not both for its debut into materiality. Many possible isotopes do not exist because the conditions of their survival are not present. Thus a peculiar primitive kind of choice already existed at the very beginning of things. Various exotic kinds of matter emerged—we can reproduce their emergence sometimes in an accelerator—but were selected against by the existing ecology of the physical world and did not survive for long. Tough objects like protons and neutrons, or intangible ones like neutrinos, can survive a great deal of wear and tear, and so they are long-lived and plentiful, as are certain elements, like hydrogen and iron, and certain molecules and crystalline structures in cooler and quieter environments.

Given matter, another open-ended process begins, of chemical recombination. Here again we find a process of variation in which the vicissitudes of a rather violent universe thrust together arbitrary combinations of chemical elements and in turn test them to destruction, leaving the survivors to survive. But in chemistry those survivors can only endure, or at best grow by accumulation, as crystals do. They cannot avoid, adapt to, or anticipate the threats of a dangerous universe. Nor, if they are especially successful at weathering or dodging the dangers, can they copy themselves so as to improve their statistical chances; yet the logic of survival in time would demand that they should. Their potentially successful form is held hostage to a particular local piece of matter; if the form could be copied to another matter, then the form might survive the enemies of matter—heat, mechanical destruction, chemical corrosion. And so yet another solution to an existential paradox emerges—life.

With life a new element enters into the iterative variation-selection algorithm by which evolution had proceeded: heredity. Life has, as it were, a double life; as matter and as a recorded copy of the form of that matter. It is more reflexive, more conscious, so to speak, than matter by itself. (Of course, as we have seen, matter is itself "double" with respect to its substance, energy: it is energy, but also a self-maintaining field structure containing the energy. And energy is "double" with respect to the space-time field, and the space-time field "double" with respect to mathematical logic.) Life not only evolved in a new way, by self-copying; it also developed in turn new forms of evolution. One of the most remarkable of these is sexual reproduction, which, instead of merely accepting mutation as part of the damage of existence, actively anticipated and promoted it by sexual recombination.

Now the biosphere took increasing control over the nonliving substrate of the planet Earth, radically altering the composition of its air, regulating its climate, setting up complex chemical cycles throughout its atmosphere, hydrosphere, crust, and perhaps even its mantle. It is thus entirely natural for an emergent and more reflexive kind of order to control and subordinate the earlier and more primitive forms out of which it evolved.

Here there is a subtlety that escapes some evolutionary biologists, who instinctively distrust any suggestion of teleology in evolution. The point is this: if the genome and nervous system of a given species are sufficiently complex to support teleology and teleological motivations (even if very rudimentary ones, such as care of the young), and if a hypothetical species is more adaptive and survives and reproduces more successfully, when it acts *as if* it possessed teleological goals, then variation could bring about such a species, and once it did, selection could help it to spread. In order to compete with such a species, other species would need to develop the same talent, of acting (and thus being motivated to act) *as if* there were teleological goals. (In just such a fashion the indicative mood of the real number series demands and implies the subjunctive mood of the imaginary number series.) After a rather brief interval of evolutionary history it would be very hard to tell whether one were living in a teleological universe, striving to become more advanced and sensitive and self-aware and concerned with the future, or whether the world around one were simply acting *as if* this were the case. And for a scientist such a difference should really be of no concern, though it might be distressing to a philosopher.

But as the competitive-cooperative ecology of the living world became more and more complex and improved forms of biological evolution accelerated the rate of speciation and ecological change, the Darwinian mechanism of biological evolution began to reach its speed limit. It takes at least a hundred thousand years for a species to develop a new capacity in response to its experience in the environment; and the whole species, or most of it, must go through that experience in order for the selective process to work. Would it not be better if something like Lamarckian evolution were to supplement Darwinian evolution?—an adaptive process that could made appreciable changes in one generation, which could use the experience of individuals rather than that of the gene pool as a whole? Would not evolution be still more efficient if alternative scenarios for the future could be tried out in a virtual world where they could do no damage, before they were actually embarked on? Would it not be better to supplement the very slow genetic diffusion of information through the species with much faster forms of communication independent of the reproductive process? Might not new forms of information storage be developed, above and beyond the genes, which would be to the genes what the genes were to the matter of which their bodies were made, or as the structure of matter is to the energy it binds?

The answer to these questions was, of course, the human species: its traditional rather than genetic way of mutating the racial store of information, its brain, its memory, its language, its cultural institutions, its imagination. Again, this new emergence was the solution to paradoxes implicit in the nature of the universe that preceded it. Survival, now revised and enlarged in definition beyond reproductive success to control and prediction of the biosphere itself, and to a richer existence within many possible time lines, required a faster acceleration of the adaptive process than biogenetic evolution could provide. Humanity is the solution to the paradoxes of life, as life was for matter, as space-time was for mathematical logic.

Of course, the irony of this process is that the paradoxes get more complex with each new solution of them; and the human paradoxes, which I have in this book summed up in the word *shame,* are the most pressing and difficult of all, especially as, unlike their predecessors, they have not yet been solved. Those thinkers who have in despair, or in denial of shame, or in fashionable cynicism, condemned the human species and its progress have not reflected that in a sense the shame of things goes all the way back: shame is most primitively the paradox of self-inclusion. If they would turn back the clock and abolish humankind (for this is the only viable conclusion to their arguments), they would be cutting off the very process of existential tension by which the universe came to be. But cannot we think differently of the unsolved human paradox?—as the open-endedness of the universe, as its evolutionary potential, as its great hope, as our chance to prove our creativity, as our solidarity with the whole cosmos in its great questioning expansion and fall, outwards into richer, more anxious, more complex, and more beautiful forms of being?

Value evolved slowly in the universe, increasing with each access of reflexivity and level of feedback, complex entities conferring value upon each other and upon the less complex by sensitively registering their presence, perceiving, eating, mating with, desiring, or loving them; and conferring value upon themselves by their increasingly intentional and planned attempts to survive and reproduce. More intense and more universal values evolved with increasing ecological interdependence, whether among whole populations of species or in those fantastically complex and swiftly evolving inner ecologies, the nervous systems of higher animals.

Between the collapse of the old Great Chain of Being and the rise of the new there fell a period in which no coherent intellectual structure existed for assigning to things the value we instinctively know they hold. (Give the most egalitarian environmentalist the choice between sacrificing a dog and sacrificing a cabbage—or a rock!—or between having for medical reasons to lose an arm or the brain, or between a chosen lifestyle and the life of a fetus, and a very clear value hierarchy emerges.) Nevertheless for some time that commonsense value system has had no rational defense, and thus our basic moral habits have been in danger of suppression by reasoned callousness. In many modern systems—Nazism, Communism, and more recently radical environmentalism or Deep Ecology—we were invited to believe that a human being was less valuable than the state, the working class, or the lives of animals and plants. In some cases the language of morality itself was used to attack our moral common sense: SS officers who collapsed under the strain of the atrocities they were expected to commit were rallied by an appeal to their moral objectivity.

Some radical environmentalists today make much the same sort of argument, asserting for instance that it is only our self-centered and traditional partiality that makes us value the lives of human beings over the lives of cockroaches, trees, or plankton. According to this view, it would be a crime to kill a billion bacteria or AIDS viruses to save a mere human life. Murder could be redefined as the harmless transformation of a human life into a rich ecology of bacteria and invertebrates. But why stop here: does not a dead rock have just as much right to exist as a living organism? Dead rocks were here before life was, after all, and have been proven natural by their long survival: would it not be moral, then, to cleanse the Earth, by a nuclear holocaust, of all life altogether, giving the planet back to the physicochemical ecology that possessed it before we, the disease of life, broke out on it?

Though the social and economic changes that destroyed the old value-giving rituals were the main cause of this crisis of value, part of the credit must go, paradoxically, to the very success of the physical sciences, which, as we can see clearly in the *Novum Organon* of Bacon, had had at their outset to fight for their very existence against rigid traditional codes of value. Science adopted a value-free ethic which worked very well for the investigation of relatively elementary and ancient objects in the world, but which was increasingly distorting when it came to biological and cultural entities. Science has, as we have seen, moved on from this initial prejudice; but the damage has been done. It is still intellectually respectable to deny any or all of the values of one's own culture, of civilization, of the human race itself.

In the absence of an objective way of determining value, we were left with four alternatives: to make value purely subjective (reader-response theory), to determine it by money and votes (Hollywood, consumer research, and the National Endowments), to make it identical with coercive political power (Foucauldian discourse analysis), or to deny its existence altogether (Deconstruction). It is the various combinations and conflicts of these alternatives that have made up the texture of public life in the last half-century. But I believe this period is now coming to an end and that we may have a chance to redeem the destruction of an old and productive, if flawed, value system, by the introduction of a new one that has corrected the errors of its predecessor and learned from the atrocities of the interregnum. The newly liberated countries of Eastern Europe may help to show the way; under their commissars they were subjected to a double dose of the cynicism we absorbed in a milder form from our own academic and bureaucratic grand inquisitors; less bribed by material and economic comforts, they may be more on their guard against it.

At the core of the new value system that is emerging is beauty. The capacity that our extraordinary self-evolution as a species sharpened, accelerated, and deepened was the ability to recognize and join in the creation of beauty. Beauty is the creative principle of the universe, the feedback process that generates an ordered world with a chaotic boundary in time. That boundary is the present moment, the culmination of the past and the source of the future; as it expands it generates broader and broader degrees of freedom, freedoms only possible and only articulable in terms of the greater intricacy of the new forms of order that are generated there. Its expansion is made possible through the existence of contradictions or paradoxes within it, and our human experience of these is of shame, tragedy, and death.

When we perceive this process at work in nature we are rewarded for the insight by the pleasure of beauty and can harmonize ourselves with it and join it in creative activity, using our evolved neurocharms as the link between the constructive energies of nature and our own more reflexive and swifter forms of creative feedback. The complex, self-similar, fractal, paisleylike, and organic forms, the complex melodies, that we find immediately attractive are a sort of logo or epitome of the deeper and stranger, more multileveled and heterarchical systems they foreshadow and subtend. The branchiness and inner articulation that such forms possess is a sign of the branchiness of the free processes that brought them about and the historical reflexivity that they embody. We see them everywhere in nature, in the whorls of galaxies, in the exquisite forms of crystals, in water currents and sea-foam, in tree branches and ferns and flowers, in the movements and ornamentation of animals, in Maori tattoos and Haida totem poles and Hokusai clouds and the imagery of *A Midsummer Night's Dream;* in Lorrain landscapes and the musical organization of Mozart's *Magic Flute* and the fantastic hierarchy of the laws of science. Most beautiful of all, perhaps, is the brain process of a human being that can experience these things; and that process is itself evolutionary, branchy, internally articulated, multileveled, and heterarchical.

If beauty is as it is described here, it must also be, as Keats said, the fundamental source and hallmark of truth. If truth is conformity to fact, and fact is the product of a feedback process that we intuitively perceive as beauty, then beauty is the way we perceive and intuit truth. This formulation is nicely confirmed by the history of science: it is quite clear that of the infinite number of hypotheses that will coherently explain a given body of observational and experimental evidence, scientists instinctively choose the one they find most beautiful or elegant. The power, economy, generality, richness, productiveness, and challenge that scientists admire in a theory are exactly the characteristics we have already demonstrated in the product and process of the universe's evolutionary feedback system: hierarchy, open-endedness, branchiness, self-similarity, reflexivity, mutual actualization and interdependence, fertile paradox, and so on.

And theories with these characteristic do tend to be true; so much so sometimes that scientists will remain faithful to them for long periods against the apparent evidence. They are so beautiful they *have* to be true. And in the cases where they really are not true, which we might compare to optical illusions, the true theory turns out to be even more beautiful, and the attractive qualities of the disproved theory often turn up elsewhere in nature. For instance, the crystalline spheres and harmonic properties of the Ptolemaic macrocosm, though replaced by the still more elegant system of Copernicus, Kepler, and Newton, return in a strange way in the harmonic and quantized electron shells of the atom. Sometimes, even, our great cultural symbols are intuitive apprehensions of the actual shapes of fundamental natural systems and processes: the snake-entwined rod, the metatron of Moses, the double-helix caduceus of Hermes, the twisted body-helix of the Hindu chakras, is an anticipation of the form of the DNA molecule.

Two possible objections arise. One is the fashionable idea that there is no progress in science, only a succession of sociologically determined paradigms, and that the idea of truth is thus meaningless. The second is more interesting: if everything is the product of a beautiful and beauty-making process, what is the point of the distinction between the beautiful and the true, and what is the status of the ugly and the merely plain and unbeautiful?

The first objection disappears with the application of a little simple logic and intelligence. There is an asymmetry between an earlier paradigm and a later one, which is that one is earlier, the other later, and thus the earlier one can be known to the later one, though the later one cannot be known to the earlier one. Thus the later one has at least the opportunity to include the ideas, perspectives, and canons of proof of the earlier, even if in a role subordinate to a reflective criticism, while the earlier cannot do so with the later. So genuine progress—which, in science, cannot mean anything other than a closer and deeper approach to the truth—must be going on; at least there is no lack of an opportunity for it to do so. If it be further objected that the later is incapable of imaginatively entering or seeing the world through the eyes of the earlier, then the same stricture must apply to the historian or philosopher of science, who claims that incommensurable worldviews succeed one another; how does he or she achieve the miracle of hermeneutic boundary crossing, while the scientist cannot? And if the historian or philosopher cannot cross the boundary into another paradigm, how does he or she know that it is different from and incommensurate with this one? Worse still, suppose this wise philosopher's views on the paradigms were to prevail: must not this be in his or her terms a step in the right direction, in other words, intellectual progress? Suppose the scientists adopted it? Would this new paradigm again be incommensurable with their former one?—if it is, then the theory must be false; if it is not, it must also be false. It is a sign that very powerful emotional forces of denial must be at work, when intelligent people can accept the kind of nonsense preached by some contemporary critics of science.

The more serious objection, that the view of beauty proposed here breaks down possible useful distinctions between the true and the beautiful, and between the beautiful, the ugly, and the plain, requires a reconsideration of the historical, evolutionary, and hierarchical aspects of the model. All of these distinctions can be kept, but in a new framework. In the evolutionary self-creation of the universe there are clear distinctions between producers, processes, and products (though any entity may be two or three of these at once). The true applies to all three, together or apart; but the beautiful applies to the continuation of the *process* of creation especially, and to the others only as conditions or signs of it. That is, a product of a beautiful process may be relatively plain in itself, even if it suggests the beauty of its creation. And the producer of a beautiful process, like the stem of a plant, may also be relatively plain in comparison to its glorious flower.

Moreover the joyful productiveness of the universe could very well generate a choking mass of dead product, or inferior or retrograde or destructive subprocesses, parodic reductions of the creative drive, that could resist, turn back, or even damage in places the beauty-making process: and here we find the ugly (and also the evil). Indeed, we have here a possible rationale for those who fear the Promethean destructiveness of the human race, and a source of valuable caution and criticism. But the answer is not to try to stop the creative process but to heighten our self-referential and conscious powers of selectiveness and use them to supplement that old, blind, ruthless, but now too slow process of natural selection. And if we are to take these powers upon us we must be prepared to accept the terrible shame of our evolution and survivorhood, the very shame that led us to deny beauty, the creative process, in the first place. And finally the only means we have for recognizing the difference between creative evolution and its destructive parodies is the sense of beauty itself. Perhaps we might suggest that the creative forces outweigh the destructive by the ratio .618 . . . to .381 . . .!

And there is even a mysterious place for the enemies, cosmic or human, of beauty. They are what can force the leap to a higher order of reflection, a new dispensation of more concrete being. This was the special insight of John Milton in *Paradise Lost,* though one finds it in various forms throughout human myth, story, and literature—the *Mahabharata* is a good example. The evolutionary drama is not a monologue (though it is not either, *pace* the pluralists, a scatter of mutually unheard voices bombinating in the void). It is a drama, a conversation, in which the participants are competing, but competing partly over the best strategies of cooperation and love; and cooperating, even when that cooperation sometimes consists in the noble adversaryhood of dialectical opposition. The nature of the drama itself is under contestation and collaborative construction, though its existence and the need to acknowledge the story up to now are established as a consequence of the asymmetry of time. And there is both the possibility and the agreement that the participants can be changed, perhaps profoundly, by each other. The deepest ugliness is not being in the wrong but denying the drama, the game itself: taking one's ball and going home.

Beauty, in the sense given it in this book, is at the core of our cognitive abilities; it is also at the core of our moral conscience. What is goodness? If we paraphrase and interpret slightly a saying of Jesus of Nazareth, it was to love oneself, to love one's neighbor (now rightly expanded to cover all beings and things), and to love above all the creative principle of the universe as a whole. Obviously one should not love everything equally. Other things being equal, we should clearly love an animal more than a rock or a styrofoam cup, and a human being more than an animal; and there are some things one should not love at all in themselves, like Nazi gas chambers (though one should in fairness love the innocent workmanship of the bricks, the crystalline structure of the iron). What, then, should determine how much, and whether, one should love something or someone?

There are two possible answers to this question. One is that one should love whatever is powerful, and the other is that one should love whatever is beautiful. Under the former we might include the instruments of political or economic coercion; and thus moral history could be defined as the competition between the love of the coercing group for their own coercive power and the desire of the coerced to coerce. Power, as we have already pointed out, consists in the ability to set in motion a linear and deterministic cause–effect sequence in which oneself is the cause, and there is as little as possible in the effect that does not derive from oneself. Thus true power results in a sequence of events in which the later state is always lesser in complexity and potential change than the earlier, because if there is something in the later state which is not derived from the earlier, then something would have escaped the determinative process. In other words, power is like a syllogism: if its conclusion contains something not in the premises, the syllogism is false. But if the object of powerful coercion were to be transformed by it into something identical to the powerful coercer, it would become a rival. Thus the transformation wrought by power must always reduce its object to something lesser than itself. A universe of power would, however complex, structured, and rich its beginning, steadily ratchet itself down into an unchanging state of simple impoverished chaos, having paradoxically stripped itself of determinative power through its very exercise; it would deconstruct itself. As we have seen, this is the exact opposite of the way in which the universe actually articulated itself into richer and richer states of complex freedom, bringing about those intricate organisms such as plants and animals and persons which we should love. Thus it cannot be power for which one loves things and people, but beauty. One might say that beauty may be a power; but that power is a paradoxical giving-over of determinativeness to others, to the future, to one's offspring, to the fruit of one's process, so that new things can arise that we did not intend. But this is a different use of the word. In its normal use power is the opposite of beauty, and as beauty is what it is good to love, then power is what it is evil to love.

Some thinkers have in recent years questioned the relationship between the beautiful and the good, using the striking image of the concentration camp commandant who goes home after a day's work exterminating people and listens to Beethoven on the gramophone. I find this unconvincing as an argument, though perhaps, as an exception, a useful reminder of the dangers of compartmentalization and specialization. It would, I think, be fair to say that lovers of beauty throughout the world generally opposed Hitler, with but few exceptions, and that despisers of beauty would have had nothing to object to in the Nazi ideology. Most Nazis, I am told by my friends who survived the Holocaust, were thugs and vandals, insensitive to the arts. But the image of the music-appreciating commandant in his smoking jacket has been taken to mean that the love of beauty is no protection against evil and may even be a kind of evil, a feverish sort of disease in itself. This image has behind it another implication still, which is that it is permissible for one of the aesthetically elect to venture into the realm of evil, boldly and self-sacrificingly exposing him or herself to the darkness and infection in pursuit of his or her art. This idea is both mischievous and silly, and invites a strict logical refutation. Let us compare the commandant's moral to his physical health. If his lungs, ribs, brain and lymph nodes, say, are horribly infected with tuberculosis, as his mind is infected with Nazi ideology, the relative health of his heart and limbs, like his love of Beethoven, should not be held to blame. Worse still, we should not in generally healthy people attempt to damage the heart and limbs in the belief that we are thereby staving off tuberculosis. And yet the attack on the love of beauty has followed much the same pseudologic.

If beauty and goodness, despite such attempts at mischief, are not detachable, what *is* the difference between beauty and goodness? It is, perhaps, something like the difference between a pull and a push. Beauty is an attractor; goodness is a duty. Goodness is the faith and will that puts us in the way of grace; but beauty is gratis, is the grace itself, gratuitous, unwilled, in an anguished but delicious near-communion with the whole of the universe. Goodness operates by policies, commandments, principles, conscientiously seeking the best angle and most economical path to catch the spirit in its flight. Beauty is the confident joining with and participation in the spirit.

Morality and goodness imply a radical contradiction between what is and what ought to be. This contradiction cannot be escaped, because in a universe of process, happening, event, and time, if what ought to be is what is, there would be no need for any new events, and the universe should instantly cease to exist (sound waves and light waves and matter waves would have to stop there, at their moment of perfection, for instance). If it did so, then "what ought to be" would no longer be "what is," because there would be no "what is." Contrariwise, if what ought to be is a process of improvement, how can one improve upon what ought to be? And again, if what ought to be is the existing state of process, but not of improvement (one version of the existentialist position), then when that aimless process brings about gas chambers, for instance, that too is what ought to be.

This paradox is right at the level of complexity of the human world, and it is unsolved. It is isomorphic with the mutual dependence and mutual contradiction of justice and mercy, human death and human immortality. It is the equivalent for us of what the statement "This statement is unprovable" is for the logical system that contains it: it points to a further breakthrough, a further integration in the evolution of the universe (one that will bring about its own characteristic unsolvable paradoxes). The paradox is at the heart of tragedy and is a restatement of the fundamental cause of shame. The only way we can apprehend it is as beauty. If we do not act upon the difference between what is and what ought to be, we neglect our moral duty; but if we so act without accepting the shame of the necessity of that difference, and without the sense of its beauty, we will become ideologues and moral monsters.

If the sense of beauty, then, is the gentle guide both to truth and to goodness, and if beauty itself, as defined in this book, is their inner principle, what are the implications for our present moment in history?

Evidently it is incumbent on us, it is our good duty, to nurture the creative process of nature and to continue it in our own work. How? Fundamentally, of course, we must listen for the voice of beauty. But the history of that creative process gives us some strong indications of where it would be best to listen—what policy will most immediately put us in the way of the muses.

First, we must educate ourselves and our children in the great neurocharms; and that means that we must find out a great deal more about them, both by consulting the ancient cultural and artistic techniques by which they were evoked and by new scientific research. This combination of cultural rediscovery and neurobiological discovery will give the next century a special flavor and quality of its own. The new age that is coming will fall into that class of historical periods that we call renaissances—periods when past wisdom and beauty are recovered, inspiring radical innovations and changes. Modernism is an old idea now, in some senses over two hundred years old. It is like the late Middle Ages in its repetitions in elaborated forms of older ideas and in its rigid doctrinal orthodoxy. Postmodernism is at best a transitional period, at worst the last gasp of modernism. The research and education that will bring in the new era are going to happen anyway. For medical and business reasons we will be exploring more and more the art of the neural-cybernetic interface, taking up where military uses, we can dare to hope, will leave off. This exploration will lead to a recovery of part of the biocultural heritage that was denied to us by modernity.

If we are to do this, however—and this is the second policy choice by which we can improve our chances of encounter with the muses—we must make a great politicocultural turn and abandon our attempts to deny the shame of our nature and history. We must accept our animal nature, the terrible sacrifices that we made to alter that nature, the validity of the higher moral and rational essences by which we judge and are judged, the shameful hierarchy of being that sets us in so special a place and makes such high demands on us, the very fact that we had our origins as suckling babies at our mothers' breasts and as hairy beasts grooming each other for fleas, and the naked self-consciousness in which we men and women see ourselves, as sexually differentiated and sexually reproducing beings destined for death. This set of acceptances involves a renunciation of that poisonous political drug, the ideology of right and left, the ideology of the denial of shame. And it means a rejection of the explanatory convenience of, and desire for, coercive power.

The third policy choice is that we should study, and allow ourselves to be guided by, the trend line of nature as it evolved and articulated itself from its immaterial beginnings, through the realms of matter and of life, and into the yet swifter and more self-reflective world of culture and consciousness. Large parts of the universe have simply not had the chance to go through much of a development, and have become, as it were, stuck in a backwater or a dead end of unchangingness; free-flying photons and neutrinos on the subatomic level, cold gases in the interstellar medium on the molecular level, protozoa and anaerobic bacteria on the organic level, the ancient family of sharks on the vertebrate level. But whenever fruitful paradoxes, high energy gradients, and new ecological niches opened up, the evolutionary process tended to produce more complex, integrated, sensitive, self-reflective, and actively transformative beings. And it has done so in an accelerating manner; and the furthest and swiftest achievement of the process, as far as we know and as far as we can responsibly act on, is ourselves. "By their fruits ye shall know them." If nature, given its head and allowed the richest field of choice and change, produces us, then we are the most natural of all entities, most characteristic of what nature is really like.

The process of accelerating evolution that the universe displays can also be described as a process of increasingly sophisticated natural technology. The bodies of even primitive living organisms are fantastically complex pieces of electrical, mechanical, and chemical microtechnology, designed for movement, digestion, self-defense, and reproduction, with the function of preserving and promoting the genes. Human technology is a continuation and supplement to that natural technology, and the acceleration of the human technology is a continuation of the acceleration of the natural.

Though the passions aroused by the issue denote our old friend the denial of shame and the mistaken nostalgia for purity, there is some justified alarm about the impact of human technology upon the natural technology that underlies it. But if we look at the trend line of natural technology, we can find a guide for human technology: human technology should become faster, more inward, more economical, more subtle, more spiritual, more self-aware and self-critical, more holistic, more hospitable to the growth of complex ecosystems and other species. As it does so it will change from being a net destroyer of biological information and (larger) net creator of mental-cultural information, to being a net creator of both.

I have deliberately used rather ugly and abrasive terms in this discussion of technology, because we need to face the cognitive and moral unpleasantness, the shame, of this topic before we can go on from there to the beauty of which it is the portal. For the secret is that technology is art, as the Renaissance knew well, and as we in our modernist metaphysical prudishness have forgotten. Indeed, there is much bad art. The answer is not to abolish art but to improve it, and to do this we must face all we have denied. The natural technology of the universe—the means that nature has found to preserve and enrich the existence of its inhabitants, living and nonliving—is the exquisitely beautiful realm of hierarchical, dynamic, interdependent form that opens itself to our senses, and which our senses and brains are so marvelously designed to perceive. It is up to us to continue our art-technology in the same spirit, but into even richer domains of complexity, ecological influence, self-reflectiveness and fertile paradox.

And this leads us to a fourth policy decision, which is theological. Voltaire said that if God did not exist, then it would be necessary to invent him. Perhaps we could amend Voltaire's premise, and say that if God, or the gods, are beginning to come into existence, then it is necessary for us to help. The universe, as contemporary science paints it, resembles nothing so much as an embryonic God, or perhaps an embryonic community of gods. The embryo has already been fertilized and begun its explosive growth in the Big Bang. It has passed from a vegetative to an active and sensitive stage, with the emergence of life. It has already developed a notochord, that infolding and self-defining mass of tissue that will one day be a nervous system; that is the brains and communities of the higher animals. Our work is to become and create a brain or collection of brains worthy of a divine mind, and to innervate the relatively insensitive parts of the universe, allowing them to communicate with us and each other, as the fetal brain innervates the fetal body. I believe that the element of the ineffable, the mystical, the intangible, the terrifyingly beyond, in beauty is precisely the emergence of that divine mind. Beauty is like the pathfinder tracks, rich with pleasure-reward peptides, which are laid down first within the embryonic human brain and which neural dendrites follow to link up with each other and wire the neurons and the body together. But to wire up the divine mind!—

surely our shame is related to our known unworthiness for such a task. But it is *our* task; that is what our neurocharms were designed for.

I have suggested elsewhere what directions offer themselves for the artistic technology or technological art of the future. Our first tentative steps in the preservation of endangered species and ecologies, and the restoration of damaged environments, is one kind of beginning. Another is the research in genetic engineering, which may one day offer the possibility of restoring extinct species by selective activation of the genes of living species that are not presently expressed, and even the creation of new species and new ecologies. Another is the seeding of dead planets in this solar system and other solar systems with genetically modified, and later, wild forms of earthly life. Another is the creation of artificial intelligence. The traditional arts can be accurately described as artificial intelligence programs designed to run on organic computers (human brains); and the use of silicon hardware, and then perhaps artificial organic circuitry, may add a startling new feedback loop to this ancient magic. Yet another direction we may take is the creation of virtual realities, cyberspaces linked up to the human nervous system.

These possibilities are really no more bizarre than the new technical resources of the Renaissance would have appeared to a person of the Middle Ages. What might truly astonish the medieval person transplanted in time into the Renaissance would have been the apparent resurrection, with a strange new flavor, of a world that he or she would have considered not only pagan, disquieting, and outdated, but extinct: the world of the ancient Greeks and Romans. If we were to be similarly transplanted into the mid-twenty-first century we would, I believe, be most surprised not by the expected innovations but by the way that all of human cultural and biological history will have become part of the landscape; by how magically corny, how shamefully old-fashioned, how primatelike and tribal we will be among the almost invisible and intangible miracles of our technology; by how slow and quiet everything will be, how improvised, how richly ornamented; how closely we will live with the animals and plants, how much in the open air; how gorgeously and formally and anachronistically clothed we will be, how morally earnest and at the same time how lighthearted, how accepting of shame and tragedy; how much also as we lived in the great pedestrian cities of the civilized past. And most of all we would be surprised by the strange, familiar, epiphanic beauty we would find there, a beauty like that of a girl going to a party in her mother's dress.